MY AUTISTIC FIGHT SONG

By Rosie Weldon

Copyright ©2020, by Rosie Weldon
All rights reserved. No part of this book may be reproduced or used in any manner without written permission of the copyright owner except for the use of brief quotations in a book review.

Published by Rosie Weldon Limited

Please note this memoir includes difficult topic areas such as mental illness and self-harm. Reader discretion is advised.

For Jenson, for being my reason.

KNEE DEEP

I had screwed everything up.

That was the thought going around and round in my head. I had turned my back on college and dropped out. So much for being 'gifted and talented' as I was labelled in high school. What good did any of my academic success do when I couldn't even turn up to school each day?

'Rosie?'

I looked up to see the career guidance counsellor, staring at me. I was sitting at the table in the middle of the kitchen. It was the biggest kitchen we had ever had, with posh worktops extending along one side and a tall fridge at the end. The counsellor sat opposite me, luckily the table was 6ft long and put some distance between us. Though, it wasn't enough to miss that her eyes were full of pity. Great, I was the college drop out.

'Hmm?' I stalled as I tried to think of anything worthwhile to say. I looked over to Mum who was stood facing me from the kitchen window. 'I need to think it through.'

That night I sat at the family computer. We had just about moved on from the PC in the cupboard and it now had a permanent desk. I loaded up MSN Messenger to talk to one of my closest friends, Lucy. I didn't need time to think it through. I knew I couldn't do any of the options I was being given: various courses, work experience or jobs that were supposed to help me get back on track.

I barely scraped through my GCSEs; things got harder near the end. I studied relentlessly from home to make up for the time I missed in class. I managed to come out with pretty decent grades. I then went back to the same school, with an attached college, to get my A-levels. It was so much harder than high school, gone were the days of routine and structure. Instead, I was in classrooms with no seating plans and there were now free periods for socialising. It all got too much and I had to bail out.

Education had always given me a plan, GCSEs, then A-levels and then university. Deciding to leave college had taken me off that path. I had no plan. Education was the one thing I was good at. What on earth had I thought, turning away from it?

Why don't you come back? I stared at the words Lucy had sent. Go back? My heart started to race. Was that possible? Could I go back? It had been six weeks since I left.

I rallied Mum for the cause and the next morning we set off to a meeting with the head of the college.

Our mission was clear: to get me accepted back into college.

We walked through the bottom gate, past the caretaker's house on the left, and towards the college block. I looked over to the track that ran behind it. On our first free period Tash and I had walked down that track to go to the leisure centre to get snacks from the vending machine. She stood in a puddle and almost hit the deck as the water went right up to her knee. It was far deeper than she had anticipated. I laughed out loud at the memory. Mum turned to give me a stiff 'this isn't the time to laugh' look.

I coughed. No, of course it wasn't.

My grin quickly fell when we reached the double doors. We walked up the stairs and turned right, into his little stamp-size office. You would think for the head of the college he would have had a bigger office. Mum purposefully sat on the first chair rather promptly, leaving me the seat next to the head. Thanks then, Mum. I may as well have been sat on his lap.

We sat there as he went on and on about how six weeks was a lot to miss, if I couldn't cope before how would I cope now? Well that was it. He wasn't going to let me back. I sat and stared at the floor, there was nothing I could do now.

Then Mum's eyes lit up with fierce determination.

'Look, I know she has missed a lot,' she said. 'But she had time off at the end of her GCSEs and she did great in those! You just need to give her a chance to prove herself. She will work hard to catch up, I know she will. Please just give her a chance.'

I looked over at Mum. Wow. She really believed in me, huh? She smiled at me and then turned back to the head, with the same look of determination as before. He sat back in his chair and looked at me.

Mum's belief gave me the strength to finally find my voice. 'I promise I'll catch up, sir. I will work hard.'

He looked at me with a furrowed brow and said, 'Okay, one chance.'

One chance was all I needed.

The next few months were as hard as the head of the college had warned. I fought to not only keep up with the current workload but work back and cover the six weeks I had missed. I knew I had doubters. I knew there were whispers behind my back that I would never pass the exams.

On my first day back, I was sitting in psychology when Mrs Finch approached me, her perfect grey bob bouncing.

'Rosie, you can go with Alex and Katie. Just watch and make notes on their presentation. Apparently, the world makes exceptions for you.' Mrs Finch quite literally looked down her nose at me. 'Good luck getting them in the real world.'

She didn't think I would make anything of myself outside of school. The 'gifted and talented' kid who was destined to fail in the 'real world'. What she didn't realise was smug smiles and shitty comments from people like her, was what fuelled me to prove them wrong.

The following day there was a morning assembly. I stood outside the common room and watched it fill. I waited until my form tutor approached. We silently nodded to each other; that was my cue that I was registered. I could leave the college block.

I was not yet diagnosed as autistic. However, I was lucky enough to be in a small rural school that met the student's needs, with or without them being labelled. I could not cope with the noise of assemblies, so my teachers didn't make me attend them.

I set off for my usual spot. I went up through the school, past the locker area and towards the right-hand tower of classrooms. The hallways were empty, the silence calming. I got to my spot and looked out of the window across the courtyard steps. I focused on finding a sense of calm before —

RING!

The doors opened and the noise built. Within seconds I was pushed against the windowsill as people bustled back and forth behind me. It wouldn't last long. I focused on the courtyard below, the trees blowing in the wind. The bustle behind me started to die down. I let out the breath I hadn't realised I was holding. It was safe for me to move again.

Everyone should have been in their classrooms for first period. I had a free period. I could have gone anywhere. I hated it. I walked up the next set of stairs towards a study room that adjoined the library, the room was for year elevens and college students only. The walls were lined with PCs and desks filled the middle. It was empty, inviting. I sat in my usual seat and got my books out. I was still behind with psychology; I would start there.

I settled into my pace of reading and note taking. A crowd of people burst into my vision. I looked up, alarmed. I saw the familiar face of my old English teacher.

'Oh. Rosie. Could we use this room?' he asked.

I didn't much care for him, he had forced me to talk in lessons, determined I would not succeed unless I participated in class discussions. Like success in life was determined by who could put their hand up in class.

'Umm. Yes. Yes. Sure. I just. Yes.' I frantically scooped everything into my bag. Uncapped pens, half open textbooks, it all got dumped into the bag.

I closed the door behind me. I had to keep it together. I had one chance. I took a deep breath and set off to find somewhere else to study.

I had just about restored my sense of balance, when I entered the tribe war meeting. That's what my brother called the arguments between my groups of friends: tribe wars. With all credit to him, it was an accurate phrase. At the beginning of college, two girls in the group, that used to be best friends, had fallen out. This had caused a line to be drawn and people to take sides, creating these tribes, as my brother called them. I thought the whole thing was ridiculous, why couldn't everyone just get along? I didn't partake in any of the friendship politics and had managed to stay friends with everyone involved. I had always managed to do that. I was amicable with almost everyone at school because I just didn't get involved in any of the drama, it all seemed very petty.

The meeting was being held in one of the college block's study rooms. The desks had been moved into one big table in the middle. There was a clear personnel divide; the two tribes sat on opposite ends of the table, with the teacher in the middle. Well that was awkward. I could have chosen a side or sat with the teacher; I wasn't sure which was worse. I succumbed to sitting opposite the teacher. I wasn't even going to talk, so I was certainly not sitting on a side.

'Rosie knows this was said, don't you, Rosie?' Lucy asked. Oh no. I had been called out for something. I wasn't even paying attention.

'Umm, I don't, I don't want to get involved,' I mumbled back. I knew I had gone bright red.

I was exhausted from the day. I just wanted this pathetic meeting to end so I could go home. The clock edged closer and closer to 3:15 p.m.

RING!

Now that bell, that one I liked. Home time.

I got home and went straight upstairs to my room. It was a small box room, but it was mine. I shut the door behind me and fell to my knees, finally caving to the pressure of the day. I backed up against my desk, knees to chest and face in hands. Through my hands I could see the familiar red and blue. I reached out and pulled it close to my chest. *'Mr and Mrs Dursley, of number four, Privet Drive, were proud to say that they were perfectly normal, thank you very much.'* I sighed into the book and fell into a world of Muggles and wizardry.

Unlike Harry, an only child, I was one of four. In our home there was Mum, then Charlie, the eldest at seventeen years old, me at sixteen years old, Jamie at thirteen years old and Jess, the youngest, at nine years old. Although most siblings spend most of their time fighting, that wasn't us. We were friends as well as siblings. Charlie was the typical big brother who always had my back, Jamie was as sport mad as me and kept me on my toes on the football pitch and Jess was my co-star for karaoke performances.

My family were a great source of comfort through challenging days like the tribe wars one. In January I was to sit my first phase of AS-level exams. Four subjects, four exams. The academics of exams didn't worry me, the change in routine however, terrified me. Each exam required the students to gather in the locker area, find their queue and get into alphabetical order by surname. Putting a hundred or so students into a confined space wasn't exactly my idea of a good time.

The first three exams were afternoon exams. I met my friends before them, and we went to the locker area together. I made sure not to lose whoever was in my class for that subject. I would stay by their side and they would, unknowingly, guide me to the right queue. Once I was in place it was following the same routine I had done for my GCSEs. I had done that, I could do this, I reminded myself.

I stood in front of Sean Williams. He was in most of my classes, which was handy. I knew my name would be just before his. My first exam was the accounting module in Business Studies. I thought back to my first accounting lesson.

Looking over at my friends work beside me I muttered 'I did it differently to you.'

'Ah,' came my teacher's voice. 'That is the beauty of numbers. As long as the answer is right it doesn't matter how you got there.'

She leant over and looked at my work. 'Yep, that answer is fine.'

I grinned back at her. So, I could do it anyway and as long as I got to the correct end point, the way I got there didn't matter. I looked down at my answer. I had the correct amount of unit sales needed to break even, but my method was nothing like my friend's.

The bell rung through the locker area and pulled me back to my place in the queue. I wasn't worried about the exam. I was looking forward to playing with the numbers until they found their way to the answer.

The fourth exam, Ethics, was a morning exam. This meant I would walk to school and meet my friends in the locker area. As I walked through the top gate, I could see the locker area. Oh no. The bell had not rung for first period yet, it would not until 9:00 a.m. We were supposed to be in place by 8:45 a.m. to enter the exam hall at 9:00 a.m. I needed to enter and find my space, not only with the exam students there, but hundreds of other students starting their day.

I stood and looked through the window. I needed to be in there. Just walk in. Just walk in that damn room and find your place. It was a college exam, I had to walk in!

I turned. I walked out of the top gate. I sighed relief. Relief for what, Rosie? Missing an exam? As I walked home the realisation started to hit. I had just failed that exam, because I couldn't walk into the crowd.

The head of the college had given me one chance.

The following day I was asked to go and see my ethics teacher, the teacher for the exam I had missed.

I walked into her classroom and stood by the desk I had sat in for high school R.E. I liked that classroom because both sides were windows. It didn't have the same feeling of being trapped that the others had. I would sit at my desk and watch people come and go to the school office. The high school nostalgia fell away when Mrs Ellis stood from her desk, crossed her arms and made her way towards me. She stopped a desk away.

'What happened, Rosie? You were ready for that

exam,' she said, her voice low.

'I'm sorry.'

'Sorry?' She raised an eyebrow. 'Don't be sorry. Let's just make sure it doesn't happen again.'

'You aren't kicking me out?' I looked up to meet her gaze.

'Kick you out?' she smiled. 'Of course not.'

She would arrange a re-sit and going forward I would plan to meet a friend at the top gate before exams.

A few weeks later I was handed an envelope with my first set of results in. I hadn't yet sat the re-take, so it was just the other three exams. While others milled around in the common area to open them together, I set off to find somewhere quiet. Upon entering the library, I made a beeline for my favourite spot, the seat next to the Harry Potter books. I loved to choose one at random, flick to any page and start reading. But not that day, that day I had an envelope to open.

I ran my fingers over the sealed line. I had been given one shot to prove I could make up for the lost six weeks. I opened the envelope and pulled out the folded piece of paper. Holding my breath, I opened it and desperately searched for the results. B in Psychology, not bad. C in English Literature, not terrible. Then my heart skipped as I registered the Business Studies result. Business Studies, A, 100%.

I had gotten 100% in the accountancy module. The lesson that felt like my time to play, had got me 100%.

How often in life did it align so clearly, what you loved and what you were good at? I looked at the 100% and promised myself that one day, one day I would be an accountant.

The more I got a grip on certain aspects of college, like the academics and sitting exams, the more I lost grip on the social side. It was taking all of my focus to get through each day. One free period the group wanted to go into town to the park, I reluctantly agreed to go. I knew I was saying no too often, studying over socialising too often. I would lose them if I didn't try to join in.

We got to the park and they started messing around on the equipment, laughing and joking with each other. I walked over to a bench on the edge of the park and looked over. It was all so natural to them, so seemingly easy to interact with each other. I willed myself to walk over and join in. If I got up, I knew I would awkwardly walk to stand by them and not know when to speak or what to say. I was better sat there, with them, but not really. Individually, I had a great relationship with them, but collectively, I got lost.

Things got even more complicated for me socially after I woke up from an unexpected dream.

I had gone to bed thinking about my future, pondering on how lucky guys were that they got to propose to girls. The act of getting down on one knee and asking a girl to marry you caught me as infinitely more exciting than being the girl in that situation.

I woke up the next morning and sat bolt upright. Oh my God. I was gay. I had dreamed that I was walking down the street holding hands with a girl, I could sense we were together, I was happy. There was no wondering, no trying to figure it out. I had never considered it before, as soon as I had, it all made sense. I didn't want to be the guy in the relationship, I wanted to be me, but I wanted to propose to another girl, that was what excited me.

A few days later I sat on my bed, back against the wall and laptop on my legs. I was running around the point in circles, before Lucy typed 'just say it, whatever it is I won't care'. I tapped my fingers against the laptop.

'I think I'm gay.' I waited for her reply.

'Well that explains why you don't fancy Zac Efron lol.'

I let out a laugh. I couldn't have asked for a better first reaction. Nonchalance was exactly what I needed when it felt like the biggest thing in the world to me.

The following week I was sitting in the common room for a free period. I didn't mind the common room when it was that empty. Blue sofa style chairs scattered the room, with only one corner occupied, by me and my friends.

The radio was playing in the background when…

'This was never the way I planned, not my intention.'

Oh no. My face burned. I lifted the textbook I was

reading to rest it on bent knees.

'I kissed a girl and I liked it,' the song continued.

I looked over at Lucy, she was joking around with Dave. I stared at the words in my book. Of all the songs to be all over the radio as I was coming out, Katy bloody Perry's 'I Kissed A Girl'. Seriously?

Coming to terms with being gay made me feel even more like an outsider from the group. Instead of being with them, dreading the song coming on, I would walk to the River Stour. The riverbank was steep, hiding me from anyone at the park.

I pulled a note out from my coat pocket. A note that I had written the last time I was sitting there, when my mind wandered to how capable I was of living a life outside of the norms. A life being gay.

I flattened the note out in my palm.

'Option A - End my life.

Option B - Accept being gay.'

I couldn't comprehend any other options. I tried to weigh both with calculated logic. I looked out at the river. I couldn't swim, so the River Stour looked hauntingly tempting as I contemplated option A. I folded it back up and placed it back into my pocket. Concrete evidence of a choice I was yet to make.

I got up and set off back across the park, deep in thought about how I still had to come out to the most important person. I had to come out to Mum. I turned up Camp Rock's 'This Is Me' to try and give me the courage I needed.

'So afraid to tell the world what I've got to say,' had become the theme song of my coming out experience.

I stood on the edge of the pavement, tapping the heel of my shoe against the curb. Mum was always late to pick me up. I got in the car and looked over at her. She was doing all this on her own. A life-altering disability had just presented itself to her and she was still doing school runs and giving everything to her children.

I thought back to the first time I saw her have a cataplexy attack.

I was stood in the kitchen doorway, looking at Mum sat at the table. We were laughing and joking when things took a sharp turn.

Mum's eyes started to twitch, and her head fell forward. Her chin was resting on her chest as she fought to breathe. I knew I needed to do something. My feet were planted to the floor as fear pulsed through me. She couldn't breathe.

I snapped out of it and rushed towards her. I lifted her head back and our eyes connected, all I could think was, 'I've got you Mum.'

Narcolepsy is a sleep disorder that meant her sleep cycle wasn't a twenty-four hour one like most of ours is. She would be awake for some of the night, and sleep for some of the day. Cataplexy is a muscle disorder that some people with narcolepsy get. It's a cruel disorder that makes her muscles go weak and can cause her to collapse, when emotions trigger it. This can be anything from fear, to laughter. A disorder that makes you scared to laugh, a cruel disorder indeed.

'Good day?' her question snapped me out of my train of thought. 'We just need to grab some bits on the way home.'

'Yeah, good day.' I wimped out. I didn't want to put anything else onto her.

I came downstairs the next morning and noticed Mum crying on the sofa. 'What's wrong, Mum?'

She pointed at the TV as she answered. 'It's on narcolepsy, how people have to accept that they can't change their disability.'

I sat with her and watched the show.

'I don't care that you have this. You're still you.' I would have given anything to take her pain away. She didn't deserve what life kept throwing at her.

She smiled at me through tears. 'I know.'

'Can you wait here a second while I get something?' I asked.

'Sure.' She reached for her tissue.

I backed out of the lounge and walked to my coat that hung behind the door. I pulled the piece of paper out of my pocket and gripped it as I walked back.

'I need to tell you something,' I said, looking at the floor.

'Oh,' she registered my tense body language. 'Are you pregnant?'

I let out the breath I was holding as I laughed. Quite the opposite.

I handed her the piece of paper. I saw her eyes fill with tears as she understood what it was saying.

'I love you, Rosie. Whatever.'

She wasn't tearful because I was gay. It was because she knew that it would make life that little bit more difficult for me. She made me promise that I would never consider option A.

I could see she was fighting her own pre-conceived ideas of my future with the need to reassure her daughter.

Coming out as gay, on top of already being socially awkward, pushed me towards a life of isolation. I quickly learned it was easier to focus on academics and pursue a dream no one could take from me, becoming an accountant. It wasn't just the lure of knowledge that drew me to accountancy. Yes, I would gladly do break even and accruals all day long. But it was also a life that I could be proud of, an achievement my family could be proud of. To be an accountant, to have made something of myself.

All of college, the social difficulties and exam hurdles, had led up to one moment. The moment when I was sitting on the floor with my laptop open in front of me. It was almost midnight on the eve of A-level results day. I frantically refreshed the UCAS university entry screen, to see if I had been accepted. I had applied to study Accounting and Finance at Plymouth University. Had I got in? Had I proved the doubters wrong?

Refresh. Refresh. Refresh. Oh, come on, it had to be soon.

Results received was now ticked at the top of the screen. I held my breath as I scrolled down the page.

Accepted.

I had done it! I was going to university.

Oh, shit.

I was going to university.

FLOATING TIN BOX

I sat on the desk chair, staring at the blank pin board in front of me. I had done it. I was at university. I put my hands down beside me and jerked them back. The chair felt strange, scratchy.

I could hear voices from across the hall. That must have been the kitchen, that would explain the strange smell. You're supposed to leave your door open. That's what I read on the university advice pages. It shows willingness to talk to people. Well, I wasn't willing. I got up and shut the door.

I was alone. One hundred and seven miles from home.

My phone went off. Looking down I realised, I wasn't quite alone. Lucy had also gone to the same university and she wanted to meet for the welcome talk later that night. Honestly, I was going to skip it. I typed back that I would meet her outside, before the talk.

I went to the talk. They made jokes about chicken nuggets and toasters, that were not funny. People laughed. Lucy spent the time talking and joking with people she had met from her dorm. She was speaking to people, how? How had she made friends in the 0.2 seconds that we had been in Plymouth? I sat back into my seat as the talk drivelled on. All that information could have just been sent in an email, maybe then I would have some clue what on earth they had said.

A couple of days later Mum phoned to check in. She tried to play it cool, but it was clear that she was worried about me.

'What have you eaten?' she asked. Classic Mum question.

'Umm.' I realised the truth as I answered, 'Well, nothing, I guess. I've been eating the biscuits you left me. The kitchen is shared. It's always so noisy.'

Well, I had gone and done it, I had kicked Mum into overdrive. Before I could protest, she had contacted the university and stated her concerns over the shared kitchen. She explained that I wasn't going to eat properly if it meant I had to use a kitchen that other people were in.

The university arranged for me to be assessed by the disability department for Disabled Students Allowance (DSA). If I got the DSA funding they would be able to put support in place.

I sat in the waiting area for the meeting. One of the lights kept flickering. The hallway was slightly too narrow, enough that people had to walk a tad too close to me. Neither of those things were helping my nerves. The problem with getting support for a disability is it relies on you communicating your problems well enough that they understand. I had diagnosed Generalised Anxiety Disorder and Social Anxiety Disorder, wasn't that enough?

'Roseanne Weldon,' a voice called. Yeah. That's my posh name.

I tried to get a grip of my mind, to see all the points I had to make. I needed this man to understand why I couldn't use the kitchen and what it would mean for me to stay in the shared dorm. I stood no chance.

'Okay, so I have devised a plan of how best to approach your time at this university and accommodate your disability needs,' was his opening line. I fumbled my bag and tried to sit down before he carried on speaking. I focused on his words. I needed to remember what happened.

He carried on explaining that he fully supported my needs and wanted me to move to a self-contained flat, that day! He said that they had allocated me a non-medical helper who would meet me the next day and talk through what help they could provide. Well that was easy. He was just handing me everything. I didn't even need to fight for it.

Whatever Mum had said to the university had worked. I had the DSA box ticked and they bent over backwards to make sure I was supported. When Mum and my older brother, Charlie, got to Plymouth we were set to move me into my very own self-contained flat. This gave Charlie the opportunity to prove, not once, but twice, that he could fit all my stuff in the back of the Rover Metro. A bet I had lost the first time around and wasn't keen on seeing his face as he repeated the feat.

The flat I was moving into was on the seventh floor. This wasn't very helpful for someone who had a phobia of lifts (they are floating tin boxes!). I put the container I was holding into the lift with Charlie and stepped back. As the doors closed, he lurched forward, pretending to try and escape from the lift. A joke about my fear of lifts, very funny.

The next morning, I woke up in my own little flat, in the centre of Plymouth. Was it ideal? No. I had managed to cope by segregating myself from everyone. Yet again, the outsider.

I rolled over to plant my feet on the floor. I had slept in a double bed. I had never had a double bed before. I reached my hand out, the divider wall down the side of the bed was close enough to touch. I scooted to the foot of the bed and reached out. The desk wasn't quite close enough to touch.

I stood and walked to the worktop the other side of the divider wall. One, two… two steps between the bed and the kitchen. I flicked the kettle on, it roared into life. It was louder than the kettle at home. I ran my hands through my hair and tried to remember my home routine. I flicked the kettle back off and clenched my hands. It was too loud. I hit my fist into my forehead. Teeth, I needed to brush my teeth. I opened the bathroom door and stood in the middle. I spun on the spot and brushed my hand against the cold ceramics. I could reach everything.

I managed to get ready and headed out to meet my non-medical helper, Sharon.

As I walked towards her, she gave me a huge grin. Oh, no. I just knew she was going to be intense. Yep, we sat on the bench and she launched into a monologue. She talked, a lot.

After what felt like forever, Sharon stopped talking. We had a plan. She would meet me outside my flat before every lecture, walk with me to it, sit with me during it and then walk me back to the flat. She was going to hold my hand through university. Great.

I stopped just inside the door of my first lecture. It was like looking out onto a baseball stadium. The rows of desks towered over the centre podium. Students jostled behind me and bumped into me. I clicked my fingers and searched for my helper's face. She was waiting just ahead. I followed behind her while she found us seats.

We sat down and she got out a notepad and paper. Umm… she was my helper, what was she doing?

'I'll just pretend to be a mature student. I'll take notes!' She grinned at me.

Oh, great. I sank into my chair and put my hand up over my face.

We walked out of the lecture and into the cold night air. The city looked kind of beautiful with the high-rise buildings against the dark sky. Except, everything looked different. I concentrated on the building across the road, I was pretty sure it wasn't there when we went in. I frowned at it, maybe it had appeared like Grimmauld Place did.

Sharon cleared her throat beside me. Right, I didn't need to figure out where we were. I fell into step beside her.

One Saturday morning, I had planned to pick up some food. I stood outside the convenience store and looked in. I had no idea what lay beyond the threshold. I didn't even know where the bread and milk would be. I took a step through the door. People were everywhere. Bright lights beamed down from above. The noise of shoppers built around me. Someone pushed past me and tutted. I wiped at my arm. The feeling lingered. I clicked my fingers and turned around. Wiping at my arm I made my way back to the flat. I would have to make do with food that didn't go out of date.

A month into Plymouth University I received a phone call that was about to bring my stay to an abrupt stop.

'I'm pregnant,' were my mum's words.

RUN, ROSIE, RUN

After Mum's phone call, I decided to go home and be her full-time carer. She has various disabilities which would have made it difficult to look after a newborn. Narcolepsy meant she would need to sleep in the day, and cataplexy would make it dangerous to hold the baby when she was feeling weak or emotional. Therefore, we set out to raise my little brother, Jenson, together.

I spent my days juggling the physical demands of being a carer and guardian, as well as the mental stress of caring. I was by her side when she fought, and beat, cancer. I was by her side when she broke to grief of lost family members. I was her carer, yet she was my rock. We became a solid team, Mum, Jenson, and I.

When Jenson reached two years old, he became eligible for fifteen hours of nursery a week. I sat on my laptop, with Jenson asleep on the sofa beside me. I tore my gaze away from him and back to the screen in front of me. An online course to become a certified bookkeeper. I looked from little man to the screen. I could use the time he would be at nursery to study.

I signed up to the course. I dipped my toe back into accountancy, while juggling the responsibilities of being a carer and guardian. This led to me craving to learn more accountancy. I signed up to do my Advanced Accounting Technician (AAT) qualification, one day a week, at a local college.

I rarely did anything outside of my family responsibilities and studying. One Saturday night, I did give in to the peer pressure from those I had been close to after high school. I agreed to meet them for a drink in the pub down the road.

I sat there as they spoke amongst themselves, not really sure what the point of me being there was. Then a group walked in the door, behind our table. I watched as they approached the bar. I recognised the girl in the hat. I was terrible with faces so I couldn't place her, but she looked familiar.

She turned and smiled at me, walking up to our table. Uh oh, she clearly remembered who I was.

'Rosie?'

'Yyep.' I hoped she didn't expect me to remember her name.

'It's Ashley,' she smiled. She knew I hadn't remembered. 'We both lived on Millers estate, we played football together.'

Right, Ashley. I did remember her.

Ashley and I went on to date. Our relationship was as awkward as that first interaction.

A few weeks into us talking I was sitting on my bed when my younger sister came into my room and said, 'Ashley is downstairs to see you.'

'No,' I said. 'I have no plans to see her. Tell her I'm not going down. I'll text her later.'

My family didn't understand. The girl I was talking to was downstairs, sat having a cup of tea with Mum. But I had not made plans to see her. I could not just see someone, unexpected. How barbaric. No, it was not something I was going to do.

Mum had to make small talk with Ashley and she still holds it against me to this day, at the level of awkwardness in my refusal to go downstairs. Well, Ashley should have text me before she showed up!

Not long after that day, I moved into my own house, down the road from Mum. Suddenly, I had my own space, yet I was in a relationship so there was someone that wanted to be in that space with me. We didn't live together but Ashley wanted to visit, a lot. I was starting to realise that relationships were far more challenging than I had ever considered. Not because it was a gay relationship, the problem was that I did not function well with people.

After a few drinks one night we got into my bed and things started to get heated between us. At twenty-one I had never had a physical relationship. I didn't like the feeling of being touched. The whole sex thing had never appealed to me.

But there I was, drunk and in bed with my

girlfriend. I was twenty-one years old and in an adult relationship, I could do it, it would be fine. The drink had helped, my body wasn't rejecting the touch as much as it normally did. But it still didn't feel right. Everything had started to close in. I felt trapped. I started to panic. Oh no, I was losing control. I needed it to stop.

I pushed her off and flung myself back into the wall behind. I could see how defenceless she was. Her eyes were full of concern, concern that she had done something wrong. I wanted to tell her that she hadn't done anything wrong, that it was me that was broken, not her.

'Do you want me to sleep on the sofa?' she asked, searching for eye contact, trying to get some kind of reaction out of me.

I stared at the bed as I answered 'yes, please.'

That wasn't the last time we tried to have a 'normal' relationship, but every time ended the same way. No matter how hard I tried, no matter how drunk I was, I could not cope with that level of touch.

This, of course, put a strain on our relationship. Not only could we not have a sexual relationship, but I couldn't even be intimate and close to her.

I got home one evening after a particularly stressful day. My days as Mum's carer were some of the best of my life, but there is no doubt that they were draining, both physically and mentally. This day had been particularly hard, I was tired. Ashley text that she was leaving soon to come over. I replied that I was tired, and I didn't want her to. She became persistent.

I could tell she was starting to lose her patience with my inability to have any semblance of a normal relationship. I didn't care how much we saw each other. I wasn't fazed by long periods of silence between us. Sometimes, I just needed space. She pushed to come over. So, I ended the relationship.

I didn't feel anything at ending it. If anything, I felt relieved. Well I had tried, hadn't I? The fact was, I wasn't built for people.

The next morning, I opened the door to find roses on the porch floor.

Oh, shit.

It was Valentine's Day the day before. That's why she persisted. She must have still driven over and left them there.

I picked them up and put them in the bin. Lesson learned. I couldn't do relationships.

We stayed friends after we broke up. She accepted me for who I was and never once asked me to change. She rolled with it as I tried to navigate being a young adult with the importance of my family responsibilities.

It didn't last long, me living on my own. I juggled the pressure of a home, when my purpose was my family. I spent more nights on Jenson's floor with my hand through the railings of his cot, than I did in my own bed. I hated having to think about everything the house needed, from food in the cupboards to bills being paid. It made more sense to live at home, so I moved back in with Mum.

On a night where Ashley and I did have plans and she expectantly showed up, I welcomed her into my bedroom. She sat on the bed as I went over and over an email.

'I need work experience,' I said, more to myself.

She got up to read it over my shoulder. I leaned into the PC and she took a step back.

'It looks good, mush, send it already.' She fell back onto the bed.

It was a generic email I was sending out to accountants in the area, to try and get some unpaid work experience. I clicked send.

After a few days I quickly lost hope of hearing anything back. At least I could say I had tried to get into the workplace.

'Rose! We need to go!' Mum called.

I closed the laptop lid and followed her out the door. We needed to go and pick Jenson up from nursery. Mum turned the engine on and went to pull away —

VRRRR!

She pulled her foot off the accelerator and looked over at me.

'What was that?' I asked.

'I think the brakes are stuck,' she said. Fourteen years of marriage to a mechanic meant Mum was pretty good with cars.

She pushed down on the accelerator again.

VRRRR!

A curtain to our right twitched.

'Mum! Stop. People are watching,' I nodded to the curtain.

'Well I need it to give,' she burst out laughing. 'We need to get Jenson!'

I looked at the clock on the dash. We had five minutes.

'Okay, go.' I sank lower in my seat.

VRRRRR!

I burst out laughing. Mum and I sat laughing as the car roared against the brakes.

'You're gonna have to walk and get him,' she said.

'Mum. I will not make it in time.' It was at least a ten-minute walk.

'Best run then,' she shrugged.

He finished in two minutes.

I got out and shut the door. Mum grinned at me as she watched me set off running. I ran up out of the estate, passed the traffic lights, up the hill past the Co-op, through the town centre, over the zebra crossing and down towards his nursery.

I opened the nursery gate and saw Donna stood with Jenson.

'I, we, the car wouldn't work,' I barely got the words out through trying to catch my breath.

Jenson ran up to me and took my hand. We walked

back home, at a refreshingly slow pace.

We walked into the lounge to see Mum sitting with a cup of tea.

'Bitch.' I laughed at her while Jenson ran up to sit on her lap.

I walked to the kitchen to get my own cup of tea. Pretty sure I deserved it more. I stood with my back to the worktop and pulled my phone out. I had an email from someone called Marshall's. They were an accounting firm just up the road from Jenson's nursery. I hoped they hadn't seen me running past like a crazy person.

The email invited me to an informal chat the following day. After showing Mum the email, I went to check my wardrobe. I hadn't expected to get any replies. I had nothing to wear.

We made an impromptu dash to Matalan, with fully functioning brakes, to grab some smart trousers and a shirt. A few hours later Jenson stood giving me a strange look as I wasn't wearing jeans.

I crouched down to his height.

'Think Rara can do this?' I asked him.

'Rara!' he shouted, jumping at me.

I caught him and stood up. Turning to look in the mirror, Jenson on my hip, I knew I had all the motivation I needed.

I returned the silly face he was pulling at the mirror and set him back down.

I dropped Jenson to nursery the following morning

and made my way back up the hill towards Marshall's. I rubbed my hands against each other and looked up at the old wooden door. Taking a deep breath, I pushed it open.

I was met by a small lobby area. An oak desk to the left, a couple of corridors off and stairs ahead. I was taking it all in when -

'How can I help?'

I turned. I hadn't noticed someone sat at the desk.

'Roseanne Weldon. I was asked to come in this morning.'

She shuffled some papers and nodded. 'Ahh, yes. I'll take you up now.'

She led me up the stairs which doubled back on themselves. We took a right turn and walked to the end of the hallway. The room we entered had a grand wooden desk that took up most of the floor space. It was four times the size of a standard desk. How could they possible reach everything on it? Did they have to circle around the edges to reach everything?

'Roseanne,' the woman behind the enormous desk smiled. 'Take a seat.'

I walked home knowing it had gone well. I had set my sights on being an accountant at seventeen years old. It was obvious to anyone who spoke to me, I loved accountancy.

I had barely got home and sat down with a cup of tea when my phone pinged with an email. I scanned down the email.

'They are offering me two days' work experience with them. Next Tuesday and Thursday.'

Mum smiled at me. 'That's great!'

I knew Mum really wanted this to work out. I had come back from Plymouth to be her carer. In her eyes she had knocked me off the course I was on to be an accountant and this was a way to get back on track.

She was wrong about it knocking me off the course I should be on. Helping to raise Jenson would always be the best thing I would ever do with my life.

Tuesday morning, I sat beside a younger woman than had interviewed me. In typical Dorset fashion it was a family run business and she was the first woman's daughter, Sian. I sat with Sian and watched her go through various excel spreadsheets. It had been a while since my high school years and my Excel skills were a bit rusty. I sat forward in my chair and tried to take everything in.

It was real. The numbers were real. The company was real. She worked through calculations of the company's finances and collated it into what would be printed and sent to them physically and digitally. I watched as it fell out of the printer onto the tray. They were completed accounts, built from the workings on the spreadsheets.

The day ended sooner than I wanted it to, and I made my way home. I burst through the front door to find little man.

'Shh!' Mum appeared from the kitchen door.

I looked at where she was pointing. Jenson was fast asleep on the sofa. I walked over and sat beside him. Pushing his hair from his eyes I watched his chest rise and fall. I could watch him sleep for hours.

Thursday followed the same routine. A day at the accounting firm and an evening sat with little man. We were sat on the floor, toys scattered around us. He stood up and walked over to his ottoman of toys. Clearly, we didn't have enough out yet. He pointed into the box.

'In there, in there,' he repeated.

He was almost three but his speech was very limited. I walked over and began picking up the usual suspects. He just kept saying 'in there, in there.'

'Out?' I asked.

He started clapping. 'Out!'

I emptied the whole ottoman onto the floor. He laughed and picked up a toy man from a car that was lost a few months before. Well, I wouldn't have guessed that one.

I started putting the toys back into the ottoman as he sat down to play. He was my number one priority. Spending two days as an honorary accountant had led me to fall deeper in love with the accounting dream. But that little boy had my whole heart. The plan was always to wait for him to start school, then pursue accounting.

A few days later that plan was about to be tested. I had received an email from Marshall's. It was a job offer. Not just a job offer, but one with full training. They would fund my AAT and put me through the qualifications I needed to become a fully chartered accountant.

I showed Mum the email.

'How can you not?' she asked.

'Jenson. You. That's a lot of hours.'

'We will figure it out.'

She couldn't fool me. Two days' work experience was one thing. This was a job offer.

I accepted the offer. They were offering me everything I had wanted since I was seventeen. Mum was right, how could I say no? The timing was terrible, but opportunities like it couldn't be missed.

I started the following Monday after dropping Jenson to nursery. If Mum wasn't well enough to get him then a friend had agreed to pick him up. It didn't feel right, it was my job to look after them, no one else's. But on that Monday, I had a different job: to be a trainee accountant.

I pushed the oak doors open and walked into the familiar lobby. I stood with purpose as I said I was there for my first day. This time she was already smiling at me, she had expected me.

She led me down the corridor to the left of the stairs, to a small office.

'This is where you will be,' she gestured to the room.

My own office. There was filing cabinets and bits of

paper scattered around. Central to the room was a desk with a PC that took up most of it.

'If the phone doesn't get answered after two rings, answer it and put it through to someone.'

She walked out, then poked her head back in. 'Oh, Lewis wants to see you once you are settled.'

I stared at the phone. It was an old fashioned one with far too many buttons. I had no idea how to use it, let alone how to put calls through. I couldn't talk on the phone, to anyone, certainly not strangers. I prayed it wouldn't ring more than twice.

I took my coat off and put it over the back of the chair, removed my bag and placed it under the desk. I was to go to Lewis when I was settled in. How long did that mean? I sat down and timed three minutes. That seemed a reasonable amount of time to settle in.

As my clock hit the 9:30 a.m. mark I made my way up the stairs. I wasn't sure where Lewis' office was. I knew it wasn't in the one at the end as she had interviewed me. I knew it wasn't where I spent my work experience as that was Sian's. I turned around and saw a third office on the left-hand side. He must be in there.

I knocked on the door and heard a deep voice telling me to enter.

He ran through some tasks he wanted me to do and we walked back downstairs to my office with piles of papers. I was to look through them and find the cash transactions.

He left to go back upstairs. I started sorting through the receipts and printed emails. A few were clear. Many were not. I could feel myself starting to sweat as I looked from the small pile I had sorted, to the big pile I couldn't place.

The phone rang. I jumped at the noise and stared at it while it rang, once… twice… and stopped. Thank God.

I turned back to the receipts. They were paying for me to be there. I had never been paid before. I had to bring to the company the value I was being paid, otherwise I was a burden. I looked at the receipts. There was nothing to clearly identify if they were paid by cash or not.

The phone rang. I jumped, again. It rang, once, twice, three times. I pushed my hands against each other as I shuffled on my seat. I was supposed to answer it. I stared at it and let it ring out. Would anyone know I had ignored it? I wouldn't get away with just ignoring it every time.

'Just popping out for lunch.' Lewis popped his head around the door. 'How's it going?' he took a step in.

'I'm not sure on these ones.'

He picked some up and glanced at them.

'Looks like cash,' he placed it on the cash pile. 'Probably card,' he placed that one on the card pile.

Looks like. Probably. He was just guessing based on the information we had available to us.

'Right, okay, thanks.'

I turned and looked at the pile left for me to make assumptions on. I heard the solid oak door shut as he left for his lunch. I had no idea when I was supposed to take my lunch, if I even had one.

Ten minutes later he returned and asked 'are you not going on your lunch? You have an hour.'

An hour. I smiled. I could go home and back in that time.

I got home and sat with Jenson and Mum. Jenson fell asleep with his head against my chest as Mum looked at me with intent.

'How's it going?'

She knew.

'Yeah, okay.' I lifted Jenson and placed him on the sofa beside me. I reached for the blanket on the back of the sofa and placed it over him. 'I should get back.'

The afternoon went the same way. I was faced with a pile of subjective papers and the fear of the phone ringing.

I looked at the clock. It was 4:30 p.m. I put my head in my hands. I just wanted the day to end. To go home to Mum and Jenson. To do what I was good at, to be where I knew I had value.

I avoided Mum's questions when I got home and got on with the housework. I wanted to make up for being away all day.

Six thirty came and I was glad for the excuse to disappear, to put Jenson to bed. We led down and I reached for 'Shark in the Park'. It was a crowd pleaser, but it would mean a second, calmer, book.

He laughed as the shark appeared each time. I breathed in the smell of his hair as his head rose and fell in time with my breathing. I was halfway through the second book when I heard his breathing change. He was asleep. I put the book down beside me and led there for a moment longer.

I knew what I had to do. But it didn't make it any easier.

I awoke the next morning to find myself on the floor beside Jenson's bed. He was sitting up on his bed calling, 'Mummy! Rara!'

I sat up and he smiled at me. He had got what he wanted; I was awake. I picked him up and headed downstairs. I placed him in his chair and set to making his porridge. I sang along to Mr Tumble as I loaded clothes into the machine. The microwave pinged and I grabbed the bowl to head back to him. Turning his seat to face me I began the spoon show. First an aeroplane. He smiled as he swallowed it.

Looking after him wasn't easy. Being Mum's carer wasn't easy. It was hard work. But I was good at it. Mum and I both had our struggles, but we were both determined to make it work. Where she was awake at night for any bottle feed, or waking up as he got older, I would do the morning routine and let her sleep. I needed a decent amount of sleep in one go, and she needed her set sleeps. We made it work and fell into the rhythm. We muddled along, the three of us.

Jenson was soon dressed and walking around behind me as I did the morning chores. I handed him some socks as we walked to the spare room to hang them to dry. He walked behind me, staring at the socks. Serious job, sock carrying.

9 a.m. came and I looked at my phone. I knew what I had to do.

I motioned shh to Jenson and hoped he would stay quiet for the next few minutes.

He began enthusiastically shushing me back. Okay, maybe that wasn't a great plan.

'Hi, can I speak to Lewis please?'

Jenson walked up to me and put his toy car on my lap. I mouthed 'thanks buddy' at him. He set off to get more toys.

'Lewis speaking.'

I took a deep breath and launched into what I had prepared the night before. 'It's Roseanne. I don't think this is going to work out. With my family commitments it's just not the right time for me to be working. Thank you for the opportunity.'

Jenson placed another toy in my lap and started clapping. I smiled at him and motioned to shh.

'Okay. That's fine. Thanks for letting us know.'

And with that I ended the call.

I would be an accountant one day. Did I even believe that anymore?

QUEEN OF MY HEART

At the end of 2013 my family and I uprooted and headed up north, to Cheshire. With Steve, Mum's partner, a firm part of the family, we settled into our new home. Jenson was due to start full time school the following September and Steve was happy to step in as Mum's full-time carer.

With all that in mind, I decided to give university another shot. Marshall's had proved that I wasn't ready to work yet. So, I stuck to what I was good at, academics. I would go to university and get the best possible Accounting and Finance degree I could. I wouldn't have the same social distractions as I did in college. I knew my best shot at a career was on the basis of outstanding academic success.

I got off the bus and walked through the back of an estate and down an alleyway that cut through. The campus entrance sat on the opposite side of a busy road. I walked further up the road and pressed the pedestrian crossing button. I used the green man a lot more than I liked to admit at twenty-four. Too many close calls with cars had forced me to accept I wasn't safe crossing busy roads without it.

On my first day at the University of Chester, I stood in the middle of the university campus. Buildings loomed over me as people bustled past me. It was freshers' week, and everyone seemed in a rush. My heart thumped against my chest.

I spotted a random door ahead of me that looked like the foyer was empty. I put my head down and made my way towards it. Once through the double doors there were bench-like seats all around the edges of the foyer, cushioned, welcoming. I went to the corner and sat down.

I desperately tried to think. The buzz of the vending machine beside me drilled into my brain. Think Rosie, you had to think. I thought back to Plymouth. Mum had contacted the university; they had helped me. I googled the disability department at Chester University and found an email address.

I drafted an email explaining that I had an anxiety disorder and had shut myself away in a foyer after panicking in the middle of the campus. I knew the odds of them picking up their emails were slim. It was freshers' and the staff must have been manic.

I put headphones in and played games. I would wait a couple of hours and then head back home.

A young woman with curly blonde hair bounded into the foyer. She walked straight up to me.

'Rosie?'

'Rosie, Roseanne, yeah.'

She gestured for me to follow her. We left the empty room behind and went out into the jungle of buildings and people. She danced through the crowds of people, while I bumped and bashed along behind her.

'Sorry. I… sorry.'

We entered a tall glass fronted building. On the right was a bustling cafe, full of chatting students. I kept my head down and half ran to catch up with her. We turned onto a staircase, at least she hadn't taken the lift. She guided us into an office and pointed to a seat. I sat in a small office and looked at a strangely happy woman, beaming at me from across the desk.

The process went similar to Plymouth's. They helped me fill out a Disability Student Allowance form and went through what help they could put in place. It all sounded great, until -

'And a non-medical helper, to —'

'No!' I cut across her.

She raised an eyebrow, '—to check in with you every week and see how things are going'.

'Right, yes, that does sound good actually,' I smiled at her sheepishly.

With a disability plan in place, bus pass sorted for the term and timetable memorised, I was ready for my first year of university. I skipped the rest of freshers' week and went straight to the fun bit: the learning.

My first lecture was Financial Accounting with a

lecturer called Lena. I had arrived early and was waiting outside the room when another student walked past me and into the room. I took that as my cue and followed in behind them.

The room was tiny compared to Plymouth. There were about twenty rows of seats behind long bench style desks. I took my seat in the back corner and watched the room slowly fill.

10 a.m. hit and the lecturer walked in. I imagined her waiting outside for the exact moment to enter. She marched down the side of the desks and took her position at the front. Turning to face us, she began, 'Welcome to the University of Chester.' She turned on the overhead projector. 'I'll be teaching you for Financial Accounting.' The module title and code appeared on the projector screen.

I watched in awe as she explained the different parts of the syllabus. She was an expert in her field, and she knew it. She spoke with confidence and purpose. She was everything I wanted to become.

Lectures like that Financial Accounting one were designed to throw information at us, and my mind was only too eager to catch it. I got to watch lecturers demonstrate their expertise while my mind danced, and my hand frantically took notes.

Lessons, however, they were not so much fun. I had taken the same tactic for my first lesson, economics, and arrived early so I could hide at the back.

'Split into groups and discuss the big four

supermarkets and their target market,' came the dreaded words.

I didn't get into a group. I sat writing my own notes while students kept turning and giving me strange looks.

I soon learned which lessons were safe and which were not. I stopped attending economics lessons after that day.

I did keep attending the economic lectures. They were in the biggest lecture theatre at Chester University, it was about half the size of Plymouth's. This was both a blessing and a curse, intimidating, but easy to hide. I headed to my favourite seat, on the back left. It was far away from the lecturer, far away from the busy areas, yet close to the door, perfect.

I was doodling when I noticed someone approaching me. They were making their way down my row of seats, towards me. What? No. Go away! That was my row, and no one was allowed in a five-foot bubble around me.

She sat right down near me, leaving just one seat between us. Well that was just rude! Clearly the row was taken. As she settled in her chair, I tensed for the feeling of being uncomfortable to hit, for her to have entered my safe zone and put me on edge. It never came. Fine. I guess she could stay. Not that she had given me a choice.

This mystery girl kept doing the same thing in different lectures. She kept sitting right by me. I was flattered - I was obviously finding the best seats in the rooms for hiding - but it was supposed to be a solo mission. If she could have pissed off that would have been great.

I tried to watch her sign her name on the register, to figure out who this intruder was, but I could never quite make it out. She spent the lectures doodling on her paper. I say doodling, it was more like artwork. The more I watched her draw and became accustomed to her being beside me, the more she intrigued me. I went to university with a clear plan, stay away from people and get a good degree. It had been a complication to college that I didn't want to repeat. But I couldn't deny that she had me intrigued. Who was this random girl who could draw trees like they should be hung in a gallery and walked straight into my bubble without shattering it?

This interest peaked one Thursday morning, during the weekly Financial Accounting lecture. I was sitting in my normal seat, by the window, when she came in to sit beside me. I was pretty used to this by now. About halfway through the lecture, the paper register was making its way around; you had to sign by your name and then pass it around. I hated this. I feared that there would be too big a gap between me and the next person, that I would need to stand up and walk to them, while people watched me. It had come my way from the mystery girl. I'm normally very careful to ensure no skin contact with anyone, I do not like the feeling it gives me. As I took the register, I carelessly let our hands touch. A buzz shot through me. What was that? I was not met by distress at the touch, instead I felt, alive? I hastily signed it and passed it on as my mind went into overdrive. This had never happened before.

I hate the feeling of being touched. A feeling of wrongness lingers where the contact once was, it leaves a grinding discomfort that I need to get off me. I try very hard, in day to day interactions, to not react, as people don't understand, and they think I'm being rude. If my hand brushes someone else's I try to discreetly 'wipe off' the feeling on my trousers. I desperately try to restore the feeling of my own skin. But there I was, certainly not feeling distressed. I had… enjoyed it?

I shook off thoughts of the mystery girl and walked through the short cut, back to the bus stop. A woman was stood there, I recognised her from my course. I approached and stood a few feet away from here, with no intention to —

'Hey, aren't we on the same course?' she walked towards me. 'I'm Marta.'

'Rosie.' I looked off to where the bus would approach from.

She would think I was rude, but it was easier that way.

'Where are you getting the bus to?' Okay she was persistent.

'Ellesmere Port.'

'Me too.' Oh no.

'The number 1?' she asked.

'Nah, X2.' Thank goodness, different bus.

She was nice, but talkative. After a day of university, I didn't always have the mental energy to navigate a verbal conversation. Though, we did soon find common ground in our dedication to the course. We talked of assignments and upcoming exams.

The next lecture I attended with her threw my 'do university alone' course off track. It was a business law lecture. I loved them; the lecturer would give so much more than what was on the slides. I headed to the back, to my usual seat.

'Rosie? Come sit with us,' Marta called to me.

I really didn't have much choice. I couldn't say no. I turned and headed to the front. The front, not exactly where I wanted to be. I sat down next to her and took my pen and paper out.

A woman leaned around Marta.

'Hey, I'm Sarah,' she smiled.

I knew those guys were friends with the mystery girl. I had seen them sat together before. She was nowhere to be seen that day. Good job, I was not ready to deal with, whatever that was.

The lecture ended and we got up to leave. They had a Managing People lesson; mine was a different day. I had stopped attending mine because it was the only thing I had on that day, and I hated it.

I always tried to bolt quickly, before most students got up, before the bustle. I would keep my head down, focus on making it through the corridors and get out into the open air, where I could breathe again. I opened the door and looked straight into her eyes, there she was, leaning against the wall opposite. She smiled at me. My breath caught. I snapped out of my daze just in time to see the next door an inch from my face. I flung my arms out and pushed the door open with slightly too much force. I laughed at myself as I walked off. What kind of embarrassing teenage shit was that?

As I walked out of the building, I heard the group behind me.

'Christine! I thought you weren't coming in,' Marta called to the mystery girl. So now I knew her name. Christine.

After that day I would sit with the group. We were sat in a small room opposite the law lecture theatre, waiting for each of our Personal Academic Tutor appointments. It was 10 a.m., my appointment was 10:30 a.m., upstairs with Lena. At just gone 10 a.m., Christine walked in and sat down opposite me.

I stood up, grabbing my bag.

'I, I should go to the meeting.'

I smiled as I walked out of the room. She scared the crap out of me.

Lena's room was above the lecture theatre we used for her Financial Accounting lectures. That explained how she always managed to perfectly time her entrance.

I sat opposite her, shuffling my feet.

'You have missed quite a lot of lessons this year?'

Yes, I had. They were horrifying and didn't aid learning.

'Yeah. They are hard to fit in with the timing of commuting.'

'Why don't you move groups?' she asked.

I looked up at her. 'I didn't realise you could do that.'

'There is a managing people lesson just after your law lecture. Should I move you to that one?'

That was the one with the group in. I could just walk from law to the managing people lesson.

'Yeah, sure,' I answered.

The following week I went to managing people with the group. I sat with Marta, Sarah and Christine. I had broken my one rule for university, don't mix socialising with academics.

'What music do you listen to?' Christine asked me.

I wished she wouldn't talk to me.

'Everything.'

'Like?' she raised an eyebrow at me, half smiling.

'I dunno, from Westlife to Eminem and just everything.'

'Westlife?'

Okay, she had my full attention. I turned to face her properly.

'You don't know who Westlife is?'

She laughed at the shock written all over my face.

'No… tell me one of their songs.'

Sarah piped in with 'Queen of My Heart.'

'Okay,' I jumped in to defend Westlife, 'that's a bad example! They aren't all like that!'

Christine looked at me, waiting for me to give her one reason why Westlife wasn't as terrible as 'Queen of My Heart.'

'Okay, fine' I conceded, 'that is exactly what their songs are like. So, what about you? What super cool music do you listen to?'

'I like bands like Hollywood Undead.'

Oh, shit. That actually did sound cool.

I regretted mentioning Westlife.

'I'll listen to Westlife if you listen to Hollywood Undead?' she asked.

She picked up her pen and wrote Westlife on the back of her hand. She put her palm out for my hand. I put my hand in hers. I tried to focus on the lecturer stood at the front, and not on her touch. I couldn't process why it felt so different. It frustrated me. It didn't make sense.

She wrote Hollywood Undead on the back of my hand and we both promised we would listen to their music.

'I will quickly run through the group presentation assignment,' the lecturer said. 'We will go over it in more detail next week.'

I stared at him as I took in his words. I moved over

in my seat, away from Christine and clenched my hand. I couldn't do a group presentation.

I got home and went straight to my room. I sat on my bed with the laptop open on my university emails. I wasn't sure who to email. My mentor, perhaps. My academic tutor, perhaps.

I addressed it to Ian, the modules lecturer. He seemed nice. Maybe I could sort this out myself. I explained that I had Generalised Anxiety Disorder and Social Anxiety, that I wasn't able to do group work, much less a group presentation.

Jenson appeared in the doorway, in his perfect little school uniform.

'Dude, good day?' I asked.

He shrugged. School, his least favourite topic.

'Wanna play Lego on the PS4?'

'Yeah!' he jumped onto the sofa in front of the TV. My room was big enough for a double bed, a sofa and TV, as well as an area that I had started to build a gym in.

The night before the next Managing People lesson, I got a reply from the lecturer. I would be given a report to do on my own, in place of the group presentation.

The following day I sat with the group in the managing people lesson.

'It's stupid,' Marta moaned. 'The people I have been put with don't even care about it.'

The others nodded, sharing their frustration

'Who have you been put with, Rosie?' Marta asked.

'I'm not doing it,' I stared at my hands. 'I'm doing a report on my own instead.'

They all looked at me with confusion.

'Disability reason,' I added.

They tried to hide the judgement, but it was there in their eyes. I had been given a free disability pass to get out of something that no one wanted to do.

I put my hand up over my face and drew the Deathly Hallows symbol from Harry Potter on my page. I ran my finger over it, it calmed me.

The first year carried on in the same systematic way. I sat with the group but kept my focus squarely on academic success. The weeks passed by and carried me through to the revision period. Exams were imminent.

I sat with the exam timetable in my hand and my non-medical helper beside me. Two weeks. Two weeks off the rails of normal routine.

I thought back to the missed ethics exam. I could not afford for any mistakes with these exams. I stared at the timetable as my breathing picked up pace.

'Rosie? Shall we go and look at the exam rooms?' my helper asked. We were sat in the friendly foyer I had found on my first day.

I nodded as tears filled my eyes. While others were dreading the academic pressure of revision and exams, I feared new rooms and noisy queues. I feared new faces and doors I didn't know how to open.

We walked across the car park and I looked across

at the doors I was so accustomed to walking through. The corridors I knew how to navigate. But we did not head to that building. Instead we took a left, went past some bike racks and I stared at an alien door. Oh no. It had some kind of buzzer intercom system. My idea of hell.

As we walked up to it, they automatically opened. Thank God for that.

I followed her through a maze of corridors, turns and doors until she stopped outside one.

'Shall we look inside the room?' she asked me softly.

I stared at the floor and nodded.

As we entered my eyes darted around the unfamiliar room. No clock. Lots of desks. Not in rows. Off-putting. Two doors in. Big windows.

As we walked back across the car park I was hit by a wave of panic. Wait! I didn't remember which doors we had gone through. I hadn't found markers to remember where to go. I didn't remember where we went!

Well next week, exam week, was going to be fun.

I got all of four hours sleep the night before my first exam. I woke up to my 6am alarm and went through the motions to get ready. Steve, my stepdad, was driving me, one less thing for me to worry about: no buses.

As the campus loomed closer, I desperately tried to scramble some sense of where I was going. I couldn't remember what it had looked like, that day with my helper.

Steve pulled up in the familiar car park, I thanked him, clarified the pick-up point and he pulled away.

I stood turning on the spot, trying to recognise something.

My usual building was in front of me, I could rule that one out. I kept turning. Sports court, bike rack, road entrance. Wait. Bike rack. There was a bike rack! I headed that way.

I got to the bike rack and then stopped abruptly. The door. The door that looked like it was an intercom, but last time had just opened. Frantically clicking my fingers, I approached it.

It opened towards me.

I walked through the miracle door and found myself in a square entrance area. There were stairs behind me and two doors on my left and right. My heart started pounding. It was 8:30 a.m. I was supposed to be outside room twenty-two at 8:45am.

Then I saw my saving grace. On the left-hand door was a notice that read 'exam in progress, quiet please.' It was not on the right-hand side door. I followed the posters until I saw the door number twenty-two with the final notice on it.

After that first exam I fell into my new temporary routine, leading me through to my penultimate exam. I needed to finish this exam promptly to then walk to Chester hospital to be with Jenson after his Grommet (ear) operation.

As I left the exam room behind, I picked up my pace to get to the hospital.

'Hey, how'd it go?' Oh, shit. That was her voice, Christine's voice.

I looked up to see her smiling at me from beside a car. So, she could drive.

Speak, Rosie. Any words will do about now.

'I. Yes. Yeah it was okay. I. Jenson, hospital.' And with that I marched off.

Brilliant. Top game, Rosie.

That afternoon I balanced revision for my final exam with Jenson. Nothing like a bit of degree revision in an NHS hospital bed.

It would all pay off in July, when I opened the email with my results in. I had not only passed the exams but done very well, I was on track for a high first-class degree. I knew I needed academic success to make up for everything else.

The next email I opened from the University of Chester was not as kind.

'As of October 2015, all Business Students will study on the new Business School campus, Queens Park.'

A new campus. A different bus route. A summer of dread.

DEVILS AND SNAKES

Returning to 'school' after a break was never easy. I had spent three months sat at my desk and the next day I was to do a new journey, to a new campus and start a new year of university. It was no wonder I found myself sat up at 2 a.m. staring at my phone. I put my phone back on charge and rolled over, I needed to get some decent sleep.

I jolted awake. I could see spiders everywhere, in my bed, on me.

I jumped out of bed. They disappeared.

My heart raced as my mind tried to cling hold of reality. It was just a nightmare; the spiders weren't real.

I sat on the edge of my bed, my head in my hands as tears rolled down my face. I couldn't even fool myself while I was asleep, I was terrified for tomorrow. Every part of my mind was terrified.

BEEP! BEEP!

I reached over and stopped the alarm. I stared, wide-eyed, at the wall. First, a quick workout.

I sat on the exercise mat that lay in the middle of

the room and began doing crunches. Throughout the summer, working out had become a big part of my life. The more you put into working out, the more you got out. I loved how systematic and rigid it was. I finished up with some push-ups and headed to the bathroom to get ready for my first day of second year.

I could do this. I had to do this.

My travel routine was the same as last year's up until getting off the bus. Instead of getting off as I entered Chester I now had to wait until it got to the bus exchange. Chester city centre's bus exchange, brilliant. I then needed to walk through the city centre to get to the side where the new campus was. This included walking over a large suspension bridge that crossed the River Dee. They couldn't have made it harder for me if they tried.

I managed to get my normal seat on the bus. The one saving grace was I got on at the first pick up point, so I generally got the same seat each time. I sat as the bus filled and the bustling got louder. I could do this. As the bus worked its way through the city centre, the grip on my own hands got firmer. Could I do this?

The bus stopped at the bus exchange. I stood up and tried to read the passengers expressions to know when to join the centre aisle movement. I was hit by fresh air as I stepped off the bus. The October air was at least, still, calming.

Before long though I was reminded of exactly where I was as people bustled around me and bus engines roared in my ears. I turned up my headphones and averted my gaze to the floor.

A bus journey, city centre and suspension bridge later I walked onto campus. I wanted to go home.

I could see the group stood outside our building. I approached them and did the customary nods and smiles. No Christine, standard. At least the day was only short. I just had to get through a couple of talks about what to expect from second year, health and safety, blah blah blah.

We entered a huge lecture theatre with hundreds of seats and sat on the front row. Awesome, just where I wanted to be, not. The first few talks were the usual introduction stuff. Then a middle-aged woman strode to the centre.

'I wanted to talk to you about the importance of the second year and the importance of Work-Based Learning' she began.

'Employers don't want just academic success anymore; it won't get you anywhere by itself. They want to know you can engage in the workplace; you can work well with people. They need to see that you have real world experience in the workplace. That is what Work-Based Learning will give you,' she said.

I stared at my hands as I willed the tears not to fall. I wasn't ready to work. I hastily wiped away the tear that escaped and began reciting Harry Potter characters in my mind.

A. Aragog. B. Bellatrix. C. Charlie Weasley. Ignore

the talk. Ignore the talk. D. Dobby.

I snapped out of the recital as her red shoes stopped in front of me. Devil Lady shoes.

Sarah, beside me, suddenly started shuffling to stand up. What was happening?

I looked at her confused as she said, 'A tour, didn't expect this.'

Damn right I did not expect this, Sarah. I did not want a tour.

We were then split into smaller groups and shown around the campus. Being hustled around between rooms and clashing with other tour groups en route wasn't really my idea of fun. I just wanted to go home. I wanted to be far away from Devil Lady and her heart-breaking truths.

I went home from day one of second year exhausted. All I could focus on were Devil Lady's words 'employers don't want just academic success anymore; it won't get you anywhere by itself'. But that was my whole plan you stupid lady. Since I realised - I couldn't talk to people like everyone else, my plan was to compensate with academic success. I thought an employer would see past my flaws if I could blitz exams. If her words were true… I pushed the thought out of my mind.

My fears around Work-Based Learning put my decision to do a placement year into question. It would be a year in full-time work in between second and third year. I had chosen it to prove to myself that I had turned away from Marshall's because it wasn't the right timing. I could hold down a full-time job. I was already starting to doubt if I wanted to do the placement when, a few days into my second year, I received an email about it. It contained details of the placement's assessment, a presentation to a room full of people. I didn't even realise there would be an assessment. Wasn't holding down a job enough of a test?

I opened my university emails. I would contact the module lecturer, just like I had in first year and they would sort this out. The module leader was Devil Lady, of course it was.

She replied within the hour.

'Everyone has to do the presentation. How do you expect to get a job at a big accounting firm? It will be good practice. They all require presentations from candidates.'

Well, Devil Lady, ever thought that I didn't want a job at one of the big four accounting firms?

I opened a new email to tell my course leader that I wanted to withdraw from the placement year. I closed the window and stared at my PC background, Jenson's beautiful smile. I had a clear plan, achieve academic success, to make up for everything else. A week into second year and it was screaming at me, my plan was destined to fail.

Work-Based Learning continued to weave itself into every facet of second year. Before I knew it, I was told that I had an interview with someone called Stacey, on Wednesday morning, to discuss my placement. Brilliant.

I walked into the familiar building of my lectures, but this time ventured off road to the second floor. I walked through the door at the top of the stairs and saw the sign 'Work-Based learning' on the left-hand door. I could see a small foyer room and then an open plan office beyond that. I froze as the panic began to set in. I couldn't walk in there. Was I supposed to walk in there? My interview was at 10:45 a.m. It was 10:40 a.m.

I found a seat in the hallway, outside of the foyer room and bounced my leg. A few minutes later a guy from my course walked into the hallway in a full tie and suit. I looked down at my jeans and shirt. My leg bounced faster. He walked straight into the open plan office and stated his name. It was that easy, if you weren't completely inept.

I watched my phone as 10:45 a.m. came and went. By 11:20 a.m. I figured I should just write this off and go home. I stood up to leave.

'Roseanne?' a voice called.

I looked around, startled to hear my name. A woman had appeared through the double doors.

'Sorry, I didn't realise you were sat out here,' she said. She had long dark hair and tried to smile at me. Don't smile at me Work-Based Learning lady, I already don't like you.

I reluctantly followed her back through the doors

she had appeared from. I was so close to escaping.

'So, Work-Based Learning is a five-week placement in which you have to do 150 hours that are signed off. It is pass or fail based on those hours,' she said, like it was the easiest module in the world to pass.

'Umm. What if… what if a student can't do the 150 hours in work?' I asked.

'Then they would fail the module,' she answered.

'And, and if they fail? What happens then?' I asked.

'Then they wouldn't pass second year,' she said.

'Right. Right. Meaning they wouldn't be able to move onto third year,' I said, more to myself than her.

'Exactly,' she smiled. No, this was not a smiling situation, lady. 'So, shall we start with potential placements?'

She found me a placement that did seem great. It was in the accounts department at a local council. I would need to attend an interview there in a few weeks. Awesome, a fake interview for a fake job, so I would not get kicked out of university.

I walked out of the interview and made my way to the bus. Christine's name lit up on my phone. My friendship with Christine pole-vaulted when we became friends on Facebook. Considering how neither of us were particularly talkative in person we would almost constantly talk online. We would sit next to each other in class, sometimes talking, sometimes in comfortable silence. Yet we 'spoke' for hours endlessly online. I messaged her back and we bitched about

Work-Based Learning while I made my way to the bus stop.

A few weeks into second year I found myself sat in a new room with a new lecturer stood at the front. We had a new module called Case Study. This was to prepare us for the 'real world' and make sure we could apply our knowledge to real life work situations. If the university told me once more that 'academics wasn't enough,' I was going to punch them in their stupid face.

I sat there, Christine to my left, as he wittered on about the importance of this module. The desks were in a big circle around the edge of the room. There was nowhere to hide, probably the lecturer's idea, some sick joke.

'Let's go around the room and introduce ourselves. Say your name and one thing about yourself,' he said.

My heart stopped. No, no, stop. Please stop. I looked at where he pointed to start. The far side opposite me. It would snake its way around and get to me, before Christine and the final person to her left.

I watched the first person do their bit. They had done it so easily. It moved on. It was making its way to me. It would get to me and I would have to talk in front of a room of people.

My breathing got shallow and rapid as my chest tightened. Adrenaline pumped through me as I sat glued to my chair. My hands faded in and out of focus as my vision started to blur. I tried to find where the snake had reached. Everything sounded muffled, like I was listening from under water. I put my hands onto my desk. Focus, Rosie. You are sat in a room full of people that are about to watch you talk.

I stared at my own hands. I could barely see them, let alone feel them. Everything felt hazy. The weight in my chest got heavier as I pushed each breath against it. My eyes rolled up and around the room as I fought the urge to pass out. The snake was now to my right, it was closing in, fast.

A blurry figure had appeared in front of me. The lecturer? Was it my turn? I turned to my right and saw the person facing me. It must be my turn.

'R… Rosie,' I stammered out as my voice broke and I put my hand to my head. I was supposed to say something else. Then I heard her voice to my left. Christine had started hers, taking the stares away from me.

I put my head in my hands and desperately tried to calm down. It's done, Rosie, it's over, breathe.

Christine looked at me, concerned, as I struggled to breathe. She leaned over, her arm going across the front of me. Her hand rested on the blank page in front of me. I watched as she positioned her pen in the top corner of my page, the muscles in her hand moving. She was close enough that I could hear her breathing. I imagined the beating of her pulse through her wrist as her hand moved on my page. I breathed into the movement and smiled as she pulled her hand away.

She had drawn the Deathly Hallows symbol.

I looked up at the lecturer and stared into his skull as I thought 'fucking bastard.'

That night I went home and straight to bed. Whatever that was in the classroom, it had taken everything out of me. All I wanted was food and sleep.

But I couldn't go home to sleep, not just yet.

I sat at my desk at home and drafted an email to send to all my lecturers. I explained my situation and that I could not participate in classroom discussions or group work. I didn't expect all of the lecturers to be okay with that. But I did hope it would weed out which ones weren't safe, in how they reacted to me asking. I sent it out to anyone that was set to teach me in second year.

I woke up to the blaring of my alarm. If it wasn't Management Accounting that morning I would have rolled back over and gone to sleep. But I loved Management Accounting, and I trusted the lecturer. She was also my course leader. I thought a lot of her.

I dragged my exhausted self out of bed and walked to the bus stop. It was almost a mile walk but it was quiet, and I enjoyed walking to my music. It helped to clear my mind and centre myself before the buses.

I got to the bus station and took my usual spot just to the right of where the bus would pull up. Far enough away from others waiting but close enough to move over quickly and get in place when the bus turned up.

The bus was due to arrive at 8:50 a.m., it was 8:30 a.m. I was always early to everything. Even as I left that morning, I thought of all the ways I would be late if I didn't immediately leave. The anxiety builds and it is easier to just set off and get there early. The lesson didn't start until 10:30am, I would get there around 9:30 a.m. This allowed me to walk into an empty room and sit in my usual seat, acclimatising to the room before anyone else got there.

Eight fifty came and went. Buses were late, no big deal Rosie. Nine ten came and went. The bus hadn't turned up. I was going to be late.

My breathing started picking up pace as my chest tightened. My feet paced up and down the length of the bench as I tried to focus my sight. I could feel the rush of adrenaline pumping through me.

I clenched my fists and released them. I couldn't slow down the rapid speed of my breathing.

My head felt light, my eyes shot around trying to focus. A bus pulled up. Did that say X2?

The people to the left of me started getting into a line. My bus was there. It was there, everything was fine.

I fumbled my bus pass out of my pocket and tried to get into line with the others. My head was spinning so fast I thought I was going to fall over. I could feel sweat over my face as I touched my forehead to try and centre myself.

I forced myself to take deep breaths as I

approached the bus door. I showed my pass and got onto the bus. Moving as far over to the window as I could so people wouldn't touch me.

What was happening to me?

I took my phone out and looked at the time. It was 9:30 a.m. I was going to be late. I couldn't walk into a room of people, so I was going to have to miss my favourite lesson.

By the time I made it through town and to campus it was 10:15 a.m. I hesitantly approached the classroom door to peer inside. It looked empty. I sighed with relief as I pushed it open and walked through.

Oh, it wasn't quite empty. I registered who it was and smiled. She could stay. I sat down beside Christine and took my pen and paper out. I put my head in my hands and stared at the front of the classroom.

That afternoon I had Organisational Management. The group had sat at the table in the middle of the room, wouldn't have been my first choice. I sat with them and watched as Kelly, the lecturer, got set up at the front. She was full of life, the sort of person that could make my life hell.

She turned and beamed at the class.

'I will run through the slides and then set you going with the group work.'

I gripped my pen. So much for thinking reaching out to the lecturers would get them to back off. She ran through the slides and I looked at my table. I was sitting with four other people, Sarah, Marta, Christine and another girl I didn't know.

The screen on the wall changed to 'Group work' and a picture of smiling students.

'I will give each group a Case Study. Either Primark or Marks & Spencer. Four of you then need to answer a question each to the class.'

My breathing started to pick up.

'Guess it's us four talking and not Rosie then.'

I looked up to see who had said it. Marta was staring back at me.

I looked at the paper in front of me, I could feel my face burning.

After the lesson I had a meeting with my Personal Academic Tutor, Lena. I thought so much of her that Christine and I had an ongoing joke of calling her 'God' as I may as well have worshiped the ground she walked on.

I made my way up to her office and stood outside. It was just a check in to see how second year was going. Could I tell her it was kicking the crap out of me and it looked like I was destined to fail the year because I couldn't work the 150 hours? Probably not.

I sat down opposite her and took in her office. There were academic texts and pictures of her family scattered around. She shared the office with another person whose desk was empty. Were they just busy or were they purposefully not there for these meetings? Maybe they had a set schedule and then-

'Rosie?' Lena repeated.

'Umm, yes?' I answered.

'How is everything going?' she asked.

'Yeah, good,' I answered. Sure, Rosie, lie to the person who is there to help you. That would sort everything out.

'How is Work-Based Learning going, found a placement yet?' she asked. Could she read my mind? Was it that obvious I was a Work-Based Learning failure?

'Fine. I have an interview for a place. It will be fine,' I lied.

She nodded at me. She knew. I could see it in her eyes. She knew I couldn't do it. I knew I couldn't do it. It was just a matter of time until the university realised, and I failed second year.

I lied my way through the rest of the meeting and said my goodbyes. I walked out of the building to be met by the pouring rain. I looked up to the sky and let it fall onto my face.

I pushed my fingers against each other, slipping in the rain-filled air, as I headed across the Queens Park bridge. Christmas time meant markets and a busy city centre to navigate through. I made it to the other side and my phone lit up with Christine's name. I smiled as I opened the message 'have you left yet? I'll be finished soon.'

Oh, thank God. I wouldn't have to walk through the city centre on my own. It was so much easier with her by my side. I replied, 'yeah, but only just. I'll come back and wait for you.' I turned on my heel and headed back to the other end of the bridge as the relief flooded through me. I would wait there.

My phone lit up and I read, 'don't be stupid. Just go home.'

Frustration crept up through me. What the hell? I wasn't being stupid. Why was it stupid?

So, I had to walk through town alone, through all the noise and mayhem. Tears met with the rain as I clenched my fist and with my head down, turned around.

Fine. I would do it on my own.

My mood improved substantially when I answered a phone call from Charlie.

'Sup?' I answered. 'You didn't reply. Thought you'd been abducted by aliens.'

'Not quite,' he said, sounding serious. 'I was stuck in a lift all day.'

I burst out laughing.

'It was horrible,' he said.

'I bet,' and couldn't help but add, 'I told you they were floating tin boxes!'

The following week I didn't attend the Organisational Management lesson. I wasn't going to put myself through unnecessary stress. A few hours after the lessons would have ended, I got an email from the course lecturer, Kelly.

'Hi Rosie, just wanted to check in and make sure everything is okay. You weren't in today's lesson.'

Well if you didn't put me in impossible situations, maybe I would turn up, Kelly.

I emailed back that the amount of group work and presentation in the lessons had me concerned and that going forward I would likely stick to just attending the lectures.

Her reply shocked me.

'I'm sorry that the last lesson was worrying for you. I do want you to know that I did have a plan for you. If you weren't in a group with more than four people, I was going to shuffle people around and make sure that you wouldn't have to talk to the class. I will always have a plan for you, when there is group work or any kind of presentation.'

I read the email over again. She would have my back in the lessons. I loved the academic content of her lessons. It was a memory test, how well the students could memorise and apply theories.

Going forward I would attend her lessons.

NOT SO SECRET ROOM

The Work-Based Learning interview at the local council loomed over me like a ticking time bomb. I knew it would show me for what I was. The night before the interview I sat on the edge of my bed. I knew I wasn't going to it, I couldn't. I rolled over and stared at the wall as the hours ticked by. I would face the consequences the next day.

I woke up and logged onto my computer. It was late, I hadn't fallen asleep until around 3 a.m. Christine's name was there in blue, she was playing some game I had never heard of.

'Morning, weirdo,' popped up.

'Hey,' I replied.

She knew I had my interview that day. She must have known I hadn't gone. The great thing about Christine was she wouldn't ask, she wouldn't push. We could talk, play games, and let the rest of the world fall away. I would face the consequences when they came, but not yet.

An email popped up from Stacey, the Work-Based

Learning lady. Okay, the consequences had found me slightly quicker than I had hoped.

The email asked if there had been a problem attending and if I needed to reschedule.

No, Stacey. I did not need to reschedule. I couldn't do it! I was at university to learn, to get a good degree. I wasn't ready to work, but that didn't remove my right to an education.

She asked me to go in and see her on Monday. I had little choice but to agree to it.

I sat opposite her and stared at her intently. It was so easy for people like her. She sat all relaxed, smiled and laughed with colleagues as they walked past her desk. Talking was so easy. Why was it so hard for me? Why couldn't I just be like everyone else and talk to people?

I set my gaze onto the desk when she started her spew.

'We will need to find you another placement if you don't want that one. You will need to do the 150 hours somewhere,' she said. Thanks, Stacey, I was fully aware of what I need to do.

'I can't do it,' I said.

'Pardon? What do you mean you can't do it?' she asked.

'What if I can't do it?' I asked. Frustration built in me as I looked back at her. Not everyone is like you, Stacey. I wanted to shout at her that I couldn't do it!

'Everyone has to do Work-Based Learning.'

'Right,' I answered.

I agreed to let her find another placement and walked out. She wasn't listening to what I was saying. She didn't realise how impossible a situation she was putting me in. I could not do Work-Based Learning, the sooner she realised that the sooner I could face whatever that meant they would do with me.

I walked out of the 'hell' room to a message from Christine.

'Do you want to come over and watch the football on Wednesday?' it read.

Go over. To her house? She was referring to the USA women's game that was on at crazy hours Wednesday night. We had been staying up late and watching them online together. But she meant actually together, at her house. I didn't go around friends' houses alone. I hadn't since I was a child and it was my best friend's house. Her house. A new place, with her family there. Wait, and it was crazy hours. Would I be sleeping there? I can't sleep anywhere but my bed, alone.

'Yeah, sure,' I typed back.

What. The. Hell. Rosie.

The night of the football came, and Steve was driving me to her house. I gripped the car door with my left hand as my right hand's fingers pushed against themselves. I was going to a new place, with people I had never met. And I was sleeping there! The thought of someone watching me while I slept sent shivers down my spine. Oh, this was going to go bad. Maybe I should have just asked Steve to turnaround and take me home. Why was I doing this?

Then I saw her. Okay, well that's why I was doing it. As she walked towards the car my breathing eased and I released my grip on the car door. She stopped and nervously put her hand through her hair. Why did she seem so nervous? She was always the cool and collected one of us. She smiled as I walked towards her and I knew that it would all be fine.

The game didn't start until 2 a.m., so we watched *American Horror Story* first. Why on earth I agreed to watch a TV show with the word 'horror' in it was beyond me. The floating head was seriously creepy.

The game started and I could feel myself feeling tired. I hadn't slept properly in weeks. Work-Based Learning was haunting my every thought, I was permanently exhausted. Agreeing to stay there wasn't exactly smart, given I was going to be up all night, unable to sleep. There was also only a single bed, which didn't bode well. Oh well, it would have been worth it to watch the game with someone else who loved women's football as much as me.

I woke up. The game was playing in front of us. Holy shit. Had I just fallen asleep? Had she noticed? I couldn't sleep in the same bed as my ex-girlfriend, drunk. Yet I had just fallen asleep, next to a girl I had been speaking to less than a year, at her house, while she was awake, and I was sober.

The game ended and we both fell asleep. I jolted awake in the night, eyes wide open staring at the ceiling. I had dreamed I was being physically dragged out of university, told I was an impostor and to leave. Great, I couldn't go anywhere to escape the hell of Work-Based Learning.

I looked to my right to see Christine fast asleep. She was the one good thing about second year. I never imagined someone could bring such happiness and calmness to my life as she had. She rolled over and put her arm onto mine as she slept. I relaxed into the feeling of her touch and closed my eyes. I fell into a deep sleep, at peace for the first time in months.

After Christmas I walked back onto the university campus with an increased sense of impending doom. I knew my time was running out. That morning I had another Personal Academic Tutor meeting with Lena. I wondered if it would be Lena that kicked me out.

I sat opposite her. Déjá vu hit when she asked, 'how is Work-Based Learning going?'

I got eye contact with her and dropped my eyes to the floor. I started to cry. I looked up at her with tears running down my cheeks.

'I can't do it,' I admitted to her for the first time. 'They are going to kick me out because I can't do it.'

'Why can't you do it, Rosie?' she asked.

'Because, because it's a new place. And new people. And I'm supposed to go into a new place and not know what I'm doing for five weeks. I can't talk to people. I can't just be in a situation and figure out what to do. I can't go into a new place. I. I can't I —'

'Rosie,' she cut me off. 'We will figure this out. You won't be kicked out.'

I looked up at her. She looked back at me kindly, yet underneath lay something else, determination? That was why I idolised her so much, she had a fierce calm about her. I wouldn't want to pick a fight with her. She was someone that you hoped was on your side.

She stood up from her seat and looked between me and the empty desk she shared the office with.

'Come with me a second?' she asked.

'Umm, yeah. Yeah, okay,' I answered. I imagined us moving to some Tony Stark style secret room.

I followed her out of the shared space and into a small glass meeting room in the middle of the corridor. Okay, this room was not so secret. She sat down and gestured for me to sit opposite her.

She lowered her voice and said, 'you have a diagnosis, yes?'

'I'm diagnosed with Generalised Anxiety Disorder,' I answered. Where was this going?

'How have you been feeling recently?' she asked.

'I don't know,' I answered honestly. 'Scared. Then nothing. Then I want to give up. It's all too much I can't, I can't—'

'It's okay, Rosie,' she intervened.

'I'm going to suggest what you should do to deal

with all this okay?' she said. 'First you need to go to your GP and explain what is happening. You need to get help for how you are feeling, medication if needed, and counselling if you want. Then ask them to sign you off as medically unable to work. With the note clearly saying that to be in a place of work would make your health worse. Then you take that note and you give it to Work-Based Learning. You tell them you can't work because the doctor said you are unfit to do so.'

That all sounded great, but it didn't stop me from failing.

'They will fail me. I will be kicked out,' I said.

'No, they won't. I will sort that out,' she stated.

I looked up at her and registered everything she had said. Doctors appointment. Get help. Get a note. Take it to Work-Based Learning. She would sort the rest out. I trusted her, implicitly, more than was probably rational.

I walked out of that meeting with a renewed sense of hope. Maybe my accounting dream wasn't quite over yet.

I did exactly as Lena advised. I made an appointment to see my GP.

I sat across from him and bumbled my way through what Work-Based Learning was doing to me. After explaining what had happened in the classroom and after the late bus, he advised it sounded like I was having panic attacks. Panic attacks, the things were nearly making me pass out. I didn't realise panic attacks could be that bad. He also said I was depressed. That was less of a shocker, I could have told him that one. He gave me anti-depressants and referred me for counselling.

'Could you please sign me as unfit for work, so I don't have to do the placement,' I asked.

'Sorry, I didn't think you were working,' he said, looking back at his screen.

Hmm, yes, I could see how it was a bit of a strange request.

'No, sorry, no I am not working. It is a placement for university. It is this placement that has caused my problems. I need to be signed as unfit to do it, so they can't make me.'

'Right, sure, okay,' he said. He thought I was completely bonkers.

I went home with my signed 'unfit to work' slip. I squeezed it as I hoped that it would be enough to stop this nightmare. I had an appointment with Work-Based Learning the following week so I would soon know.

Before I could find out Stacey's response to my note, I had a Sage lesson on the Friday. Sage was an accounting software and the lessons were insanely boring. Click here, type into this box. But they were with Christine and Sarah and we always had fun laughing at how ridiculous the lessons were, so it was worth turning up to.

Christine hadn't turned up yet. Not exactly unusual, I would estimate at about a 50% chance of attendance from her in second year.

My phone lit up with her name. Little shit, messaging me to rub it in she was still in bed no doubt.

'I've been in a car crash. I won't be in today,' the message read.

My heart stopped. Car crash. Was she okay? I needed to know she was okay. I had an urge to stand up and just walk to her. I didn't even know where she was. I could do nothing to help her. But I had to know she was okay.

After what felt like hours, she explained that she was just shaken up, with bruises and cuts but nothing serious. Her car was a write off.

That was the moment I realised I loved Christine. It wasn't that I didn't want my life to be without her, I already knew that. It was the overwhelming urge to know of her safety, it was so primal. It wasn't logic, it wasn't a feeling I was used to, it was love.

She didn't come back to university for a few days after that. As she walked into Management Accounting the following week, I let out a breath it felt like I had been holding since the crash text. I could finally see she was okay. I joked with her about her lame, scratch-like, injury on her hand.

It didn't scare me, loving her. It just was. It was as easy as breathing. I didn't want a relationship; I had tried that once and wouldn't again. Maybe that was why love, without a relationship, was so easy, no expectations. Our friendship was one that many would never understand, intense at times, a roller coaster of peaks and dips. But it worked, for us.

After the lesson we walked together into town. She made her way to the bus station and I continued onto the other campus. I had a Work-Based Learning meeting to attend.

I walked up the stairs with the note in my hand. I willed myself to stay strong, to show the note and explain that I couldn't do it because of medical reasons.

After she called my name, I followed her into the usual open office mayhem. I sat down and put the doctors note on the desk between us.

'I... Umm,' and then I proceeded to pat the note.

Great job, Rosie. Patting the note definitely helped.

Stacey picked up the note and I saw the moment she registered what it was.

She stood up and took the note with her as she walked off. Where was she going? Please come back, Stacey. Don't go and get security to drag me out.

She came back and said 'can you come with me? We need to go and see the head of Work-Based Learning.'

Oh, God. That was it. I had waited months for them to tell me that failure at Work-Based Learning meant I could no longer continue my degree. Tears started to fall.

I followed her into a small room where an older man sat in a suit. He smiled at me. I wished he wouldn't. If he was the head of this hell of a module, then he was Satan to me.

We all settled into seats and he began by saying 'Stacey says you are unable to do the module.'

I stared around the room in shock as the tears got heavier. I had been telling Stacey that for months! It was only with this note that she was taking me seriously.

'Yes,' I answered. 'I can't do it because of my disability. I have a note.'

'I see,' he said, taking the note of me.

'So, what will you do instead?' he asked.

Instead? What would I do instead? I had no idea. What was my plan B, did I even have a plan B? I was told I wasn't allowed a plan B.

'I have been contacted by Lena and the head of Rosie's course,' Stacey said. 'They are creating a placement within the university for her.'

Well that had done it. I began hysterically crying at everything that was happening.

'I thought I was going to be kicked out,' I said honestly.

The suited man smiled at me, 'why would you be kicked out?'

'Because, because I can't do the 150 hours at work,' I said, looking from him to Stacey. 'I was told if I couldn't I wouldn't pass second year.'

He looked from Stacey to me and then reassured me that I wasn't going to be kicked out. He would speak to Lena and my course head to make sure a plan was in place for me to do the 150 hours within the university. Lena advised that their plan was to create a job role within the faculty department.

I walked out of the meeting and the most profound relief washed over me. I put my face in my hands and sobbed. I wasn't going to be kicked out.

I looked through my hands and realised I was stood in the middle of the corridor and people were looking at me. I should just… head home.

A LIFELINE

A week or so passed after the embarrassing note patting incident. I received an email from my course leader asking for me to go in and see her. We were mainly revising in lessons, so I wasn't attending very much. I was pretty sure she was going to reprimand me.

I knocked on her door, she smiled and invited me in. Her office was also shared, even the course heads didn't get their own offices.

'How are things, Rosie?'

I was sick of being asked that question. Things were terrible. Life was kicking the crap out of me. But I was still sat there, wasn't I? So yes, give me a medal or something.

'Yeah, okay,' I answered.

'I have been sorting out this Work-Based Learning placement. It will be a research position for the Accounting and Finance department. We want you to analyse our position in the market in the context of a competitor analysis report,' she said.

'Thank you. Thank you so much. And Lena, I know she helped sort this,' I said.

She smiled at me. 'So, I guess that would be okay, that placement?'

'Of course! Yes, sounds amazing!' I said, genuinely excited by this research position.

'Lena will lead the position and check in with you throughout. She will email you to schedule the interview for it. Just so it is all the same as the rest of your cohort,' she explained.

I went home that night and started looking up competitor analysis, it was all so interesting. At 3 a.m. I accepted defeat and went to bed; I had the interview with Lena in the morning.

The interview went really well. I would spend the five-week placement in the library, researching and writing a report. The final report would be given to the department as an official document they could use to progress the course's national standings. I couldn't wait to prove myself to both Lena and my course head.

That weekend I had plans to celebrate the renewed security on my degree, with my brother's birthday celebrations. The siblings were up from Dorset and we were heading into Chester. Clubs weren't my favourite place, but music and a drink were exactly what I needed.

I stood in the club as the music blared. My siblings scattered around me, dancing, drinking, laughing. There was no better sight than real laughter on the face of a family member. It was exactly what I needed after an uphill fight through second year. I would give everything to exams, and then to Work-Based Learning. Right in that moment, I wouldn't think about what came after that.

Later that night I walked back into Mum's surrounded by drunk siblings joking and bumping into each other.

My phone lit up with Christine's name, 'Rosie!'

Uh oh. She had named me, that was never good.

'Yeah?' I typed back.

'You can't just tell me that!' she said.

I scanned the conversation. What had I said? Oh. Oops. I told her I was in love with her. I was so comfortable with it I hadn't realised I had mentioned it. I had said that although I was in love with her, and did not want to date her, that if she could get with someone as cool as a celebrity then it would make my life a lot easier.

I told her I was in love with her in April, I had known since January. So really, I did pretty good not mentioning it until then. Points should go to me for that.

She did not see it that way. She lost her shit at me. Whoops!

I woke up the next morning to a headache and stream of messages from Christine. She clearly thought it was a drunken text that I didn't mean.

'Dude, chill,' I sent to her 'It's not a big deal. I did

mean it but let's just forget it. The whole point of the joke was that I didn't want anything to change.'

Luckily, for my sake, things did go back to normal between us.

The next week I stood outside of Lena's office, hopping from one foot to the other as I squeezed my hands tightly. I was due to get feedback for my Work-Based Learning interview. I looked at my watch, 11:59 a.m. It was scheduled for 12 p.m. I am nothing if not punctual. I would wait one more minute. Lena didn't scare me, I felt okay around her. But the process of knocking on a door terrified me. I'm not really sure why.

12:01 p.m. Lena has thrown you a lifeline and saved your degree. I willed myself to knock the door.

I knocked and Lena smiled at me through the glass in the door, gesturing for me to enter. I flustered with my bag and settled into the seat opposite her. I smiled at her and then set my gaze on the desk as she began talking.

She went through the interview and gave some truly helpful feedback on how I did. Then she said the comment that changed the course of my life.

'The biggest thing that you need to work on, is holding eye contact with the person interviewing you.'

I could feel myself going red as I raised my gaze from the desk, to lock eyes with hers. Nope. Didn't like it. My eyes shot off to find somewhere else to settle as I mumbled that I struggled with eye contact. Lena assured me it was just something she felt I should be aware of and could possibly work on.

As I walked out of her office, my mind whirled and my fingers tapped against themselves. I really was bad with eye contact. I looked down at my hands as they tapped and tapped, uncontrollably against themselves. I knew what this was all signs of.

I got home and sat at my PC. I opened Google and typed in 'signs of being autistic'. I sat up all night and I saw my own experiences reflected back at me on the screen.

I eventually stumbled across the #actuallyautistic tag on Tumblr. I was hit by a rush of emotion as I read an autistic person joking that if they were wearing gloves they couldn't hear very well. What an absurd thing to say. What a strangely accurate thing to say.

I had no doubt I was autistic. There had been rumblings of connections between autism and myself when I was younger that I had brushed off. Just because I was quiet didn't mean I needed a label as significant as autism. But things felt differently that night. I looked back through the last two years of torment through the lens of autism. I saw the panic attacks on the bus as triggered by sensory problems, the failures of group projects to someone unable to communicate properly.

I was also hit by the realisation that if it was autism, if I was autistic, then I could not change that. I would be like that forever. During my autism search I found a statistic I would never forget, only 16% of autistic adults are employed full-time. I would circle back around to what I wanted to do with that information, after exams.

There was something that I did need to action from the meeting. After admitting I never followed through with the medication for depression and anxiety, she made me promise that I would.

'If you want to give yourself the best shot at working after university, you need to get the help you need,' she had said. She had a point. The problem was, medication terrified me.

I was a week away from my first exam, but I followed her advice and made the appointment. He prescribed anxiety medication that should help stop the panic attacks. I didn't much believe in miracles, but I figured it was worth a try. They wouldn't be dispensed for a few days so I'd be a few exams in when I could try them.

I committed myself entirely to revision. I ate, breathed and slept theory, formulas and calculations. It had always frustrated me that everyone just expected me to do well in exams. I didn't wake up on the morning of the exam just knowing it all. I worked my arse off for every exam I sat. These would be no different. Whatever happened after, I would commit in that moment. I didn't know how else to be. I didn't know how to give anything but 100%.

I sat the exams in the same separate rooms as first

year. I was familiar with them which was a huge bonus. I came out of the third exam feeling content with what I had done. Exams were like letting my mind run free, I could just tell the paper everything I had studied. I loved the methodology and rhythm of them.

The first week of exams was done and I geared up for the next week. The next week had my favourite, the Management Accounting exam, and one of the hardest. I focused on the hardest and tried to nail group accounts, which I had always struggled with, as it seemed less logical, and more random.

My favourite, Management Accounting, came and went. I thoroughly enjoyed playing with the numbers. Management Accounting questions had become my go to for fun revision when I started to worry about performance in other areas, so I knew the content inside out. The next day I was to sit Case Study, the consolidation module.

I woke up to my blaring alarm and turned it off. Case Study I could do. It was applying theory, combining it with logic, and solving a problem. I quite liked it. I looked at my desk to see the packet of tablets sat there. They had arrived the day before and I was due to take my first that day. They were for anxiety and panic attacks, they should help. I thought of my promise to Lena, to fight for my future, and I swallowed it.

Two hours later I was sitting in the Case Study

exam scribbling away. My handwriting was terrible, but it was hard to slow it down when my brain went so fast. I didn't want to miss anything.

Everything started to blur on the page. I sat back and looked around the room, trying to refocus my eyes. I felt dizzy. I put my hand on my chest. Normal heartbeat. This didn't feel like a panic attack. I squeezed my eyes shut and reopened them. The room started to spin.

I stared at the clock until it came into focus. Twenty minutes left. I looked down at the exam paper. I was on the last question. I held my head steady with my left hand and tried to remember the question. I went back to scribbling; I wrote anything I could think of that remotely made sense to the topic area. I couldn't re-read the Case Study now; I was going to faint if I tried. I tried to end the answer with some kind of logical conclusion and put the pen down.

I put my head in my hands and tried to breathe deeply.

The exam invigilator came and collected my paper and told me I could go. I slowly stood and picked up my stuff. I walked to the door and made my way out. The toilets were nearby. I blinked as I tried to see in front of me. I pushed through the doors and saw the sign to the toilets. I shut the cubicle door just in time as I fell into the wall of the cubicle. I slid down the side and onto the floor. I tried to lift my head and find my phone, but I was too weak.

I rested my head against the toilet and closed my eyes to try and stop the spinning. I couldn't help but think that my life was joke. It felt like every time I got back up and tried to fight back, I was beat back down. I opened my eyes and managed to get some semblance of focus.

I opened my phone and text Mum that I had basically fainted in the toilets and I'd be with Steve soon.

'Do you want him to go and find you?' her reply read.

Absolutely not, abort mission, Mum, abort mission. That was the motivation I needed to slowly get up. I held on to anything I could and made my way out of the building. The road leading out of the car park had railings down one side. I gripped onto it and slowly walked towards the campus exit.

I finally got to Steve's car and my phone went off, it was Mum.

'Did you take those tablets this morning?' she asked.

Right. The tablet. Why hadn't I thought of that? I must have reacted to the new tablet.

I got home and managed to get into bed. A weight started pushing against my chest as my breath caught. I coughed against the tightness which made the breathing worse. I text Mum who had gone out for the afternoon and said what was happening. She said either I phone the NHS helpline, or she would come and take me to A&E. The medical helpline it was! I had the Financial Accounting exam the next day, I was not going into hospital.

The NHS helpline advised that the drugs had lowered my blood pressure too far but should be out of my system by the morning. They said if I was worried then I should go in and be checked. Nope, I was staying right there on that bed. I hung up the phone and looked around. I needed to revise.

I could see my revision prepped on the desk. I had never been so grateful for my own organisation.

I sat up in bed and my eyes rolled their focus around the room. I purposefully fell off the bed onto the floor and crawled over to the desk. It seemed a safer option, to stay closer to the ground in case I fell.

I got the books, pen, paper and calculator and shuffled back to the bed. I heaved myself back up and took a minute to catch my breath. I felt like I had run a marathon. I propped the book up in front of me and got paper and a pen. I held the calculator and the weight of it pulled at my arm. I placed it down beside me and pressed the buttons into the bed.

I rested my head back against the pillow as my neck screamed at me for a rest. Every part of me felt like it was falling apart.

I revised like that until the early hours of the morning before falling asleep covered in textbooks and paper. Luckily, my alarm had previously been set and woke me up the next day for my final second year exam.

The next day I was exhausted and weak, but okay. The people on the advice line had been right, it seemed to have left my system. I took my usual migraine tablet and knocked the others off the desk into the bin. Not today, thanks.

After the exams were all done, I decided to pursue the autism diagnosis. Perhaps I needed people to understand why I was the way I was. The journey to diagnosis began with a trip to my local GP. I went in armed with examples of autism traits and was ready to fight my corner. I didn't need any of that. After saying I felt I was autistic, and wanted to be assessed for this, the GP set the process in motion.

The first step was to answer a questionnaire that I received in the post. It asked for signs of the most common autism traits, such as how I interacted with people and my experiences with change. I filled it in and returned it. I then had to wait to see if I was through to the next round. I felt like I was being given challenges to prove my autism, if I was autistic enough then I would get through to the next round of mission autism diagnosis.

I passed with flying colours and made it through to the next and final stage, a two-hour long assessment. How to diagnose an autistic person? Make them talk for two hours and watch them crumble? Thanks, NHS. The letter I received, thankfully, outlined the plan. I would need to attend with someone who knew me well, preferably throughout my life, Mum fit that bill. We would then be split up and individually have to answer questions from different professionals. Thankfully, that appointment was not for a few months, standard NHS.

While pursuing the diagnosis I hadn't given up with the treatment plan. Lena was fully supportive of me having counselling and doctors' appointments around my Work-Based Learning placement. I was put on tablets that were similar to the migraine ones I took every day. The difference was I would take three a day and they would be slightly higher in dosage, but, as I was repeatedly reassured, not as high as the ones I had previously tried.

The triggers for the panic attacks were less now that I was working alone for five weeks so it was hard to get a judgement of whether the tablets were helping. That was, until Lena sent me an invite via email to a staff training course for faculty members. I wasn't even proper faculty, this had to have been a joke.

Another email came through after the invite.

'You don't have to do this. Just thought it would be a good way to push yourself. And give you something to write about in the end of module assignment.'

She wasn't wrong. After the module I would have to analyse my placement. This would give great material for that. Doing it would be like an investment in my academic success for the module.

I was spending my days playing with data and

analysing trends. Though I knew that the little bubble Lena had created for me was not something I would find after graduation.

I accepted the invite and started planning for the staff training. I google mapped the route and looked at the front of the building. It was an old-style building by the river in town. At least I recognised where it was. The plan for the day outlined sections on health and safety and staff wellbeing. Lena had assured me I wouldn't need to participate; it would just be watching boring power points.

On the day of the training I managed to find the building and got myself inside. It was empty, most students were off revising by that point. I took out my phone and checked the room number. It was in room 217. That meant the second floor. I had recently learned that and happy to put it to good use. In front of me was a huge staircase that twisted up and away from me. I headed towards it and made my way up.

I found room 217 and stood outside. I was early, typical. I pushed my fingers into themselves and looked around. I could feel anxiety rushing through me, but I didn't tip into a panic attack. I wasn't sure if this was because of the medication or the counselling, but I was glad to stay in some kind of control.

Eventually, people started turning up and going into the room. I followed suit and placed myself at the back of the room.

The room started to fill, and, wait, was that? Kelly,

my Organisational Management teacher, walked in. She smiled and waved at me.

Please don't sit next to me, please don't sit-

She sat next to me.

'Rosie! What are you doing here?'

I explained how I was doing my placement for the university and it was an exercise to introduce me to what work life would be like.

'It's going to be pretty boring,' she joked. So I had heard. 'But it has to be done,' she went on, almost like she had realised she was talking to a student.

'I really want to tell you something,' she began, but seemed to stop herself.

Okay… this day was getting weird.

'You got 97% in your exam!' burst out of her.

Ninety-seven percent. I stared at her in shock. I had almost aced a three-hour, end of second year exam. Ninety-seven percent.

'It's not official so don't tell people,' she continued. 'You did amazing. Can I use your exam to show other students? Without your name, of course,' she asked.

'Yeah, yeah of course.'

The morning got significantly less weird, and more boring, as promised by Lena. After what felt like an eternity of power points, I was making my way home. I sat on the bus pondering the 97%. Maybe she was joking. Surely, I hadn't got 97%. How would I feel if I did? I wasn't sure it was a good thing. It felt more like the world was laughing at me. Telling me, 'look what you could achieve, if only you weren't so broken.'

UNHAPPY BIRTHDAY

I sat staring at the screen that showed my second year results. 80%, 84%, 87%, 92% and 97%.

I continued to stare at them. So, Kelly wasn't kidding about the 97%.

I hadn't done Work-Based Learning, not properly. What was the point in those results, when I would never be able to work? I closed off the page, text my family my results, and carried on playing. The results didn't mean anything to me, they wouldn't change anything. 97% was an impressive result, I couldn't deny that. But it wouldn't make up for not being able to talk to people.

If my time since exams was in a movie, it would show a fruit as it wilted, while I stared at the wall. The slow realisation that my future was coming for me. The emptiness as I saw nothing but darkness ahead.

PING!

'Congratulations on your…' the email pop-up said.

On my what? Fully expecting a spam email about a prize draw I clicked the pop-up.

'Valedictory award' the email heading finished.

What on earth was a valedictory award?

The email went on to outline I had been awarded the J. Andrew Wood Prize for Work Related Studies as a valedictory award. I pulled out my phone and sent Christine a message, 'Did you get some email about an award from the uni?' I asked.

She replied instantly with 'Nope, why?'

I looked at the email. This had to have been a joke. Work related studies, so Work-Based Learning. I had not won an award; it was some kind of set up.

I showed Mum and Charlie the email, then googled it to try and find out if it was even a real award. It did all check out. I sent back an email thanking them and advising I didn't want to collect it in person.

I sat and waited for a response that would apologise for the confusion and explain I hadn't won the award. It didn't come.

Two weeks later the award arrived in the post. So, apparently it wasn't a joke. Well, if it was, someone had gone to great lengths to follow it through. Mum wanted to frame it. I wanted to burn it. I didn't want it. I didn't deserve it. I threw it on my bed and turned my back to it.

I woke up and looked at my phone, July 17th, my twenty-fifth birthday. I threw my phone to the floor. I didn't give a crap about my birth or any other day that celebrated my excuse of a life. I was twenty-five, on a downhill road to thirty, and what had I achieved?

Nothing. Every day was a sorry excuse for the oxygen I wasted, and I wasn't going to celebrate it.

My whole life I had just wanted to be normal, to walk the normal path of job, marriage and home. I was never going to be able to work, I sucked at relationships and I would never be able to live alone. So, what was the point?

Jenson came crashing into my room. He ran and jumped onto the bed, half landing on me.

'Happy Birthday, Rara!' he shouted, with a huge grin on his face.

I held onto him and rested my forehead on the side of his head. 'Thanks, buddy,' I said.

He started to pull my arm, trying to get me to go downstairs and open his presents. Luckily, I had fallen asleep fully dressed the night before, so I gave into his smile and let myself be pulled out of my room.

An hour later I had gritted my teeth through the present giving and was sitting back at my desk. I sat back in the chair and stared at the wall.

At midday Mum walked in to find me staring at the wall.

'Everything okay?' she asked.

I sat up and shuffled around, moved my mouse onto a game.

'Yeah, yeah just got lost in thought,' I replied.

'We are leaving now, to go down south. You sure you don't want to come with us?' she asked.

'No. I'll be fine here.'

Birthday or not, I was better off on my own.

I went downstairs to kiss Jenson goodbye and watched as the car pulled away. After locking the front door, I made my way back upstairs.

I walked through my door and stood looking at the room. It was my birthday. What a joke that was.

I clenched my fists and stood rooted to the floor as frustration built in me. I didn't want to be like this! I didn't want this life!

I turned on the spot and smashed my fist into the wall. Pain seared through my knuckles. It felt… good. It felt… satisfying. I swung back and punched again, harder. I fell to the floor as I held my hand. My knuckles had gone red. I was going to break my hand.

I wanted more pain. I needed more pain. I looked around, looking for another way to feel that rush of pain. I opened my desk drawer, looking for anything sharp. A stack of staples shone back at me. They would do.

I held them in my right hand and looked at my left arm, tattoos exposed as I was wearing a T-shirt. I put the sharp edge of the staples against the top of my forearm and pulled it across. It barely scratched my arm. I took a deep breath and raised the staples above my arm. I held my breath as I slashed them down across my arm. A red line followed the staples as it started to bleed. I smiled as pain shot through me.

I did this another four times before I suddenly stopped. I opened my right palm where the staples lay.

I became awash with shame as I realised what I was doing. It was self-harm. I was self-harming.

I dropped the staples and pushed back in my chair. I got up and grabbed a hoodie, throwing it on to cover my arm.

I walked downstairs to get some food. I was not that person, I would not self-harm. I opened the fridge and looked at the food Mum had left for me. At the bottom of the fridge stood various bottles of alcohol. Huh, maybe that would help. I grabbed two bottles and went back to my room.

I resumed my position of wall staring as I drank. It was my twenty-fifth birthday. What a joke.

The summer continued on in a similar fashion. I wore jumpers in the summer because I regularly succumbed to the staples. It was a Friday morning and I had, yet again, refused to go out with the family. They were off to visit the beach and I had opted to stay home.

I sat holding the card Christine had sent me on my birthday. The words 'Love you' stood out from the rest. It was the first time she had said it. But, if she meant it, where was she now? A few days after my birthday she had stopped replying to messages. We weren't talking and I could feel the distance between us.

I put the card back in my desk drawer. Screw her.

An email popped up on my screen saying 'Chester University third year…'

Fear shot through my numb state as I clicked into

the email and it finished 'timetable'.

Third year was coming for me and I had no way out. Third year would end, and I would still have no way out. I was a student on track to do academically well. I was a student on track to crash and burn as soon as university ended.

I wanted it all to stop. I wanted out.

Tears rolled down my face as I felt the gravity of those thoughts. I wanted out. I wanted my life, over.

I opened my drawer and pulled out the panic attack tablets. They were blood pressure tablets. I knew the effect too high a dosage had on me last year. Would it just feel like falling asleep?

I began popping out the tablets onto my desk. How many would I need? I popped out the whole packet until I had a pile of tablets in front of me.

If I swallowed those, my nightmare would be over. My family were sick of me in my current state, I would be doing them a favour. I would be saving them, and myself, from the inevitable crash, post-university.

I put one in my mouth and swallowed. I put the second in and swallowed.

I stopped and stared at them. I didn't want to die. I didn't want to die!

I picked them up and screamed as I threw them across the room. They hit the wall and scattered across the floor.

I picked up my phone and called Charlie.

As soon as he answered I said, 'I need help'.

A week later and I was sitting on Charlie's sofa watching the Olympics, the women's football was on. He had arranged with Mum and Steve for me to be taken down south to spend some time with him. Not to talk about things, not to analyse what had led me to that point. But just to spend some time with my big brother. It was exactly what I needed.

I put thoughts of Work-Based Learning and my future to the side as I laughed and joked around with him.

I jumped up from my seat with my hands over my face.

'Shit!' Christen Press had just skied a penalty. If Sweden scored, then USA were out of the Olympics.

I sat back down on the edge of my seat. The Swedish player walked up to the spot and I leaned forward.

The Swedish player blasted it to the keepers left and it hit the back of the net.

I stood up from my seat and looked at Charlie.

'Well. That's it. The Olympics is cancelled.'

Charlie began laughing as I got up and left the room. I walked to the kitchen to get a drink and returned to find him watching the Swedish celebrations.

'It's cancelled, Charles! Turn it off!'

I didn't watch another second of the 2016 Olympics after that. Heartbroken.

I went back up north with a clearer mind. I would

continue to pursue the autism diagnosis, I needed to understand why life felt like a constant uphill battle. I would try to enjoy third year. Academics were my safe haven and the thought of what came after was taking that from me. I would enjoy third year, enjoy one more year of academics. It was also one last year of regularly seeing Christine. She had messaged me not long after I got to Charlie's, but I had always known our friendship was bound to implode one day. I wasn't sure it would survive after university. One more year. Then I would face what came after.

SUPER AUTISTIC

The day of the autism assessment had come. I was not only going to be interrogated for two hours, but it would have serious ramifications on my life. Part of me wanted to be told not to be ridiculous, of course I wasn't autistic. Part of me wanted to be told that I was autistic and be given an explanation for my ways and the struggles I faced every day.

As I sat in the waiting room with Mum, I thought over my life, trying to remember all the details. It was like revising for an exam on my own life.

My name was called and we both got up to enter the small office. I slowed down to ensure Mum entered first, she would do the initial greeting while I scoped out the layout of the room and the seating situation. I headed for the seat off to the side, leaving Mum the one directly opposite the man who had welcomed us in, ha, score.

He seemed nice. He explained that it was just an informal chat about my life experiences and how I felt about things. That I would first go and talk to his colleague while Mum spoke to him, then after an hour we would switch. Two hours of non-stop talking, fun.

A new woman entered the room that I was to follow. I was twenty-five years old and did not want to leave my mum's side in this unknown territory. I sat down beside this woman. The chair I was supposed to sit on was against her desk, far too close to another human for my liking. I nudged it away as I sat down.

'Describe a typical day in your life to me,' she asked. What kind of ridiculous open-ended question was that?

'What day?' I went back with, trying to clarify what she wanted.

'Well, any day,' she answered.

'Yeah, but what day?' I repeated. 'A Monday?'

Well this had started well. It was going to be a slow and painful hour.

'Yeah… sure… a Monday if you wish,' she answered, looking at me very confused.

Now that was clarified I launched into Monday's routine. 'Well Mondays I start uni early and I'm there all day. I get up at half five and I work out. Monday is abs day, so I do abs. Then I get dressed, I would have put my outfit on my chair ready to get into after working out. So, I get dressed. Then I go downstairs and get my cup of tea and take my tablet. Then I go back to my desk and do the online puzzle that updates each day. Then I am at uni all day so I…' I looked at her. I had talked a lot. Did she not want this much information? I should stop.

'So that's umm... that's basically my Monday,' I stopped.

She was writing notes down on her paper. I had probably said something wrong. I squeezed my hands and started to count the squares on the floor. I liked floors with a pattern.

'Do you have any friends at university?' she asked.

'Yeah, kind of. I mean I met someone at university that I am very close to. But we don't really talk at uni. We talk online more, just kind of sit together at uni,' I replied.

'Are you in a relationship?' she asked.

'No,' I answered. 'I tried it once, didn't work out. Never again.'

The questions went on and on. Interrogating the parts of my life I didn't tend to advertise to people.

The hour was finally up and I was told to switch with Mum and be interrogated by the other doctor guy. I sat down in the office we first entered and looked around. This wasn't his everyday office, there were no personal objects.

'Do you tend to misunderstand jokes or sarcasm?' he asked.

'I get jokes if they are funny. Most people's jokes aren't funny,' I answered. 'I am sometimes sarcastic, but I don't normally realise when someone else is being sarcastic.'

'Does that cause problems with people?' he asked.

'No,' I answered honestly. 'Either I ask them, or they should just tell me. If people actually said what they meant, then it wouldn't be a problem, would it? People just never say what they mean.'

'Do you like things done a set way?' he asked.

'Well there's only one best way to do something. Find that and do it every time, right?' I said. His face was saying he did not agree. He scribbled more notes on his paper.

I looked around the room. No squares on this floor. I didn't think this was going very well.

'Okay, I think we are done here,' he said after an hour of talking.

I was exhausted and just wanted to go home. Mum walked back through the door and smiled at me; I was glad to see someone familiar, safe.

We took our original seats and they left to confer in the next room.

'How did it go?' Mum asked me.

'Yeah, okay,' I answered. 'I'm tired.'

She smiled at me in the way only a mother could. She already knew I was exhausted.

They walked back in and sat opposite us.

'Usually we would advise that you wait until you get the official report before we give any insight into the outcome,' he said. 'But we are both in agreement that you exhibit many autism traits and a diagnosis will follow once the write up and report is done.'

So, I wasn't just autistic... I was super obviously

autistic. Wait. I was autistic. Autistic. Autism.

I wasn't sure why I was so surprised at the outcome. I had pursued the diagnosis. I already knew I was autistic. This was just clarifying it so people would understand me. So why did I feel like I had just had a label stamped on my forehead? A label I wasn't sure I wanted anymore.

I went back to university for third year and let the disability department and my course head know that I was autistic. I also let Lena know. She showed zero surprise. I was pretty sure she had already figured it out through the Work-Based Learning dilemma.

It didn't really change anything at university because I was lucky enough to have lecturers that wanted to support me, with or without a diagnosis. It did, however, change how I looked at myself. I knew that I, once again, was on a journey to accept something about myself. I no more wanted a life as an autistic than I had wanted one as a gay person when I was a teenager. But there I was, a life as an autistic person was what I had.

The third year Case Study module included a group work project. After a meeting with the course head I had surprisingly decided to do it. I know, I shocked myself too. I could choose my group, and I didn't need to present. A plan was put in place, that I could bail and do it individually, if it got too much.

I was sitting next to Sarah when we were told to choose our groups.

'You with us?' she turned and asked.

'I. I can't present though,' I answered. The course leader had agreed I didn't need to present. But that would mean someone else in the group would need to present my slide as well as theirs. I was pretty sure no group would want me, and I would just do the individual report.

'Are you kidding me? We don't care. You will be so much help with the rest of it,' she smiled.

The morning before we were due to give the presentation, I was sitting in a separate room off the library. Christine was to my right, Sarah and Marta were sat opposite me. I wasn't even giving the presentation, yet my leg bounced like crazy as anxiety pulsated through me.

'To fiddle with,' Christine whispered, pushing a pen towards me.

I picked the pen up and started playing with it. It was a welcome distraction to the nervous energy running through me.

'Okay, Rosie. Explain these one more time,' Sarah pointed at one of the slides.

I had not only done my slides but done a lot of research for the other guys. I had helped Christine with her ratio slide and explained what each of them meant for the company we had chosen.

I knew I had done more than I needed to. But I was desperate to make up for the fact that I couldn't help with the presenting part. None of them wanted to do it, yet I had a disability free pass.

Being autistic, for me, meant I couldn't talk to people, but I was great with data and analysis. I decided to work harder in other areas to make up for the guilt I felt in not being able to help them present.

The alarm on Sarah's phone went off. We all got up to head down to the classroom where we would present. Well, I wouldn't present. I would watch as they presented.

I stood awkwardly by the computer podium while they all readied to deliver the presentation. I felt like a spare part, watching them do their thing.

Christine walked over to the middle to do her bit. I could have recited what she needed to say, I knew the material inside out. She froze as she reached the current ratio. She had forgotten why it dropped in the previous year.

They invested in short term investments, Christine. They invested in, just say it!

I wished I could put the words into her mind.

Christine stared at Sarah, who turned and looked at me.

'They invested in short term investments,' I whispered.

Sarah then whispered it to Christine who said it aloud.

Sarah smiled at me. Okay, maybe I was of some use.

The rest of third year continued on in a similar

fashion. I accepted my flaws and worked hard to compensate with my strengths. I had chosen the tax module because I thought my analytical mind would take well to it. What I didn't account for, was potential problems in attending the lessons.

The tax lesson was at 2 p.m. on a Monday. I was already with the group because we had lessons that morning together. I sat with them while they ate, I couldn't eat in different places, and then headed up to find the room with them. Except, the room was full. There was a lesson in the same room, just before tax.

That wasn't usually something most people would think about, but I immediately saw what was going to happen. The corridor would fill with tax students. They would line the sides of the walls and build in numbers. The time would come for the classroom to empty. A room full of people would push through an already full corridor. Then the tax students would all, simultaneously, try to enter the classroom and find seats.

I attended a handful of lessons and then gave up. I got pushed around in the corridor and ended up sat in seats I wasn't comfortable with. After one particularly horrible lesson seated in the middle of the room, I called it a day on attending tax lessons. So, I set out to teach myself the tax module. No easy feat.

For completely different reasons I also barely attended any Financial Accounting lessons. For the simple fact that I did not trust the lecturer. They were no longer taught by Lena, instead by a new, far less understanding woman. She had asked me a question, in front of the class, on the first day. Not only had she asked it, but upon me staring at her like a deer in the headlights, unable to talk, she persisted. I knew the answer, but I couldn't talk. I hated her for it and lost all trust in her. I attended a handful when I knew Christine and Sarah would be there but quickly started skipping more than I attended.

Management Accounting continued to be my safe haven and audit would never know that my great attendance in that module was because it was after Management Accounting.

The thread of thought they instilled in second year's Work-Based Learning continued through third year. I tried to block out the constant talk of preparing for our careers. I would face it after exams.

JULY 7TH

Exams were over. I wouldn't find out until July how I had done. But the job search would start immediately.

It was the moment I had been dreading for years. Was I employable? Could I hold down a job? I guessed I was going to find out one way or the other.

I sat at my desk, equipped with cup of tea and notepad.

Job searches are notoriously difficult for graduates. I knew I had to throw enough mud at the wall that some would stick.

I polished my CV and set to loading it up to various recruitment websites. I google mapped and researched public transport to draw up a list of locations I could apply to. I then started firing out applications. It was fun, systematic.

My days soon became filled with working out and researching job options. I balanced the pressure of finding work with the release of running on the treadmill. Part of that pressure was answering all the phone calls I was getting, as many important ones were now from unknown numbers.

To remove as much of the uncertainty as possible I kept a record of everyone I contacted. This included important information on the caller as well as potential scripts to help me answer their questions. It also included scripted responses to basic questions such as my date of birth or email address, to prevent any embarrassing silences while I processed how to word the response.

One of those phone calls came from a recruitment agency, asking me to meet them in Liverpool. It sounded great, I agreed to meet them. The following Thursday, Steve would drive me to an office in Liverpool where I would meet with the agency worker.

Wednesday evening I sat on the edge of my bed, staring at the floor. I knew I couldn't go the next day. Who was I kidding? I couldn't walk into some unknown office and meet a new person to discuss going into work. Tears escaped as I felt reality crushing around me.

I got up and closed my door. I took my phone out to text Steve that it was cancelled. I then took my glasses and belt off and dropped them to the floor as I knelt on my bed.

My face fell into my hands as my chest hit the duvet.

I cried. I cried out of embarrassment. I cried out of fear. I cried at the realisation I couldn't do it.

Devil Lady was right. My old English teacher was

right. I was nothing without academics. I thought back to the night I researched autism. Only 16% of autistic adults are in full-time work. I guessed I wasn't meant to be one of the 16%.

I cried until I couldn't breathe.

I cried until I fell into a hopeless sleep.

I woke up the next morning to puffy eyes and a heavy heart. It had become impossible to ignore the crushing reality of the Mount Everest of a situation I faced. What was I going to do, if I couldn't even attend a meeting about interviews, let alone do the interviews themselves?

I put the job applications on the back burner and settled into a workout and gaming routine. I didn't even have my results yet. I could put it all off for a little while.

RING RING!

I looked down at my phone. Unknown caller ID.

I threw caution to the wind and answered while I opened my phone call spreadsheet.

'Hello,' I very poshly said.

'Hi, can I speak to Roseanne Weldon please?' a stern voice asked.

'Yeah, speaking,' I responded, curious to know who this was.

'Hi Roseanne. I'm phoning from the Bank of America. Do you have time for a quick chat?' asked the stranger.

Why on earth was the Bank of America phoning

me? Shouldn't they be phoning people in America? No, I did not have time for, nor want to 'chat' with some stranger.

'Yeah, sure. How did you get my details?' I asked.

'I found them on Indeed. I am phoning to ask you to apply for a job at the Bank of America.' She stated, getting straight to the point.

'Yeah, no. I'm autistic and an investment bank just wouldn't work for me.' I just wanted to get off the phone and go back to the game I was playing.

'That's no problem. I can assure you that won't stand in your way at the bank. Why don't I send some information on the role over and you can email us an application, should you wish? We are keen to have you apply,' she pushed on through my rejection.

'Okay, yeah I'll take a look,' I gave in to her pressure. Also, just please let me put the phone down.

The next morning, I was mindlessly scrolling through my emails, while waiting for Tomb Raider to load on the other screen. I saw the Bank email sitting a few lines down. I glanced at Tomb Raider; it was doing an update. I guessed it couldn't hurt to see what this Bank thing was about. I clicked into the email and scanned through the job specification. Product control analyst… profit and loss… substantiation of data… analysing trends… It was being an accountant for trading accounts.

Okay. I would give it to the pushy lady, she had my interest. It did sound kind of cool, and she said herself being autistic wouldn't matter, right?

I filled out the form and sent it back.

I had done it just in time for Tomb Raider to finish loading. I could get back to what really mattered: Lara chasing clues from her dead father.

The following morning, I walked downstairs to grab a quick cup of tea before going back to my bedroom.

'Tea, Mum?' I looked to her, sat at the kitchen table.

'Yeah, please. I need a sleep, but I'll have a quick one first. Heard anything back from any applications yet?' she asked softly. She of all people knew my inner turmoil at what lay ahead of me.

'No, nothing. What will happen, if I can't do it?' I asked as I flicked the kettle on. 'What happens if I'm not good enough for anyone to want me?'

'Rose. They would be stupid to not want you. Look at your grades and how hard working you are. A good employer will see past the things you can't do. You want to do accounting, not present classes. Have you thought about looking for part time work?' she asked.

I stared at the sugar as I tipped it slowly from the spoon into the cup, the grains edged closer and then fell in. Yes, I had thought about part time work, a lot. I wasn't sure it would be any easier. Less hours, but essentially the same hurdles.

'Yeah. Not sure I'd be able to do that either though.' My heart started feeling heavy again as I sighed into my cup of tea.

'If you do part time, you do part time. If you can't work yet, then you can't work yet. Whatever happens, we will figure it out,' Mum said.

'I know, thanks. I just. I need to work. I need to do it.' I stared at the floor.

'I know, Rose. I know.'

A few weeks later I had helped Lara Croft solve her clues, and I had racked up the kilometres on the treadmill. I was sitting playing Sid Meier's Civilisation against Christine, it's like The Sims for geeks. She would always build a better empire and it was very frustrating. I had an important decision to make, attack the barbarians or flee.

PING!

No, email. I was busy building an empire.

The subject heading caught my eye. 'The Bank of America invites you to…'

Fine. I clicked the pop up and continued reading.

'…a candidate recruitment day at the Chester site.' It went on to outline that the day would consist of groups of six doing different tasks and being whisked off at different times for interviews and tasks.

I closed the email. Well that was that. I had done what pushy lady wanted and filled out the application, but there was no chance of me going to a day like that, doing group work and god knows what.

I went back to building my civilisation and chose to attack the barbarians. I had nothing to lose at that point.

As our game went on, I couldn't help but let my mind wander. Every way I turned with these job applications I hit a brick wall. I knew I was good at accounting and finance. But it was all surrounded by so much crap I couldn't get through; I stood no chance.

RING RING!

Unknown caller ID lit up on my phone.

'Hello.'

'Roseanne? I'm calling from the Bank of America.' I recognised her voice. It was the pushy lady.

'Hi, yeah, speaking.' I definitely should not have answered the call.

'I just wanted to check in and see if you received the email, inviting you to the recruitment assessment day?'

'Yeah, I did. I can't do something like that, so I won't be able to go,' I answered honestly. I was beyond beating around the bush. I am autistic and some things just can't be done. Assessment days were a big no no. Devil Lady at university had always said that I would never get a good job without being able to do them, I guessed she was right.

'Oh. Okay, that makes sense. Let me go back and talk to the Bank and see what we can do,' she said.

See what they could do? I had no clue what that meant but I just wanted her to leave me alone.

'Sure, yeah, okay.'

'We really do want you to go through the application process, Roseanne. I'll get back in touch when I find out what can be arranged.'

I put the phone down and shook my head. It was getting ridiculous. I couldn't even do interviews, so unless she had some miracle cure for anxiety and way for me to communicate, this was a waste of everyone's time.

The next morning I woke up early, restless and uneasy. I put on sports clothes, grabbed a drink and headed to the garage.

As I pressed start on the treadmill the belt jolted into action and began running underneath me. I watched the black line that connected the belt whizz past, again, and again. I placed my bottle in the holder and pressed play on my running playlist.

I was greeted by Skepta: 'whenever you feel like letting go, and you've got your back against the wall, hold on.'

I stepped onto the moving belt and fell into a rhythm as I increased the speed. I reached a running pace and stared ahead. My feet fell onto the belt as the music consumed my mind. Breaking Benjamin rang through the garage: 'I will not bow. I will not break. I will shut the world away. I will not fall. I will not fade.'

Twenty-five minutes later I had a clear mind, gathered my things and headed back into the house.

I went through the motions of showering and getting ready for the day. I had fallen into the ease of a stress-free routine. I gamed and worked out for most of my day.

I sat down at my PC and settled in. I would be there most of the day. Music on one screen and a game the other side, perhaps some Grand Theft Auto V that day. That way I could do races while listening to music. Christine wouldn't log on until much later, she was pretty much nocturnal, basically an owl.

I scanned my emails as other applications were opening, Amazon, eBay, EE, the usual suspects for sending me rubbish. Until I saw 'Interview stage candidate'. It was from the pushy lady. Part of me wanted to just delete it. I was sick of this rat race making me feel crap about myself. It was never going to work out.

I reluctantly clicked into it.

The email explained that she had gone to the Bank and explained I couldn't do the assessment stage, for disability reasons. They had proposed that instead of doing that, I would do a phone interview and then in person interviews.

A phone interview. Was that a joke? Absolutely not.

I kept on reading. She explained that the phone interview would be with her. Huh, not so bad. She had attached the questions she would be asking me.

Okay. So, it was with her, she seemed okay at least. Pushy, but understanding of my disability. I would also know the questions, so it was less like a conversation and more like a verbal test. Tests I can prepare for. Tests I can research and anticipate.

The phone interview would be on Thursday. In two days' time.

I looked for the attachments. The first outlined competency-based questions and the second outlined technical knowledge questions. I opened the technical knowledge questions. I was met by words like 'derivative swaps' and 'options and future'. I had a vague understanding of these but had never properly studied them.

I opened Google and threw it to the other screen. I searched for 'options and futures'. Up popped explanations of financial hedging, the Black-Scholes model and risk management theories. I read, then opened a new link, then read some more. The Black-Scholes model gave a formula for giving the price of the option. That was cool. Swaps were like trade-offs between risks. My mind whirled as it connected these things to my own business and accounting knowledge.

My stomach rumbled. I sat back in my chair. It was 3 p.m. Christine was online, I hadn't seen her name pop up. I had run that morning and was yet to eat anything.

I took in the state of my screens and desk. Windows were open and scattered across both screens, notes written haphazardly across my desk.

My mind had been gripped by the financial theory.

I opened up the email and replied that I would like to take the opportunity of the phone call interview and I would speak to her on Thursday.

I had two days. Two days to prepare for the interview.

First, I needed food.

The morning of the interview came around quickly. I had sheets of paper all laid out in front of me. On the left-hand side were the competency-based questions and answers, on the right the technical ones. I had written scripts for all my answers. A third section underneath my keyboard had general research on the Bank in case she threw me a general curve ball question on the company.

The phone rang, at exactly 11:30 a.m., as planned.

I answered the phone and stuttered on my first greeting. Brilliant start, Rosie.

As I settled into the conversation, I found myself reeling off the information I had absorbed on futures and options. The competency questions went better than I expected, I recited my scripted responses on teamwork and ability to prioritise tasks.

'Thanks, Roseanne. That's all my questions for today. I will be in touch to let you know if you are through to the next stage.'

Next stage... how many stages were there?

I leant back in my chair and breathed a sigh of relief. That was actually not terrible. It was like being given free rein to info dump all this cool information I had researched the past two days.

Then it hit me. I wanted to make it through to the next stage. The technical material and even my research on the Bank itself had made me want this job. I wanted to do accounting for an investment bank. Well, I never thought that would happen.

The next week was spent refreshing my emails and checking my phone for missed calls. For the first time, I really wanted to hear from the pushy lady.

One morning, I finally heard back. I received an email congratulating me and inviting me to the next stage, which was two face-to-face interviews. Seriously, these stages just kept coming. It was like climbing the never-ending staircase in Super Mario.

The interviews would take place the following Tuesday, four days away. My mind started to race, I needed to sort out what I was going to wear, how I was going to get there, wait, where even was it?

The next four days were spent doing those things, frantically Google mapping Chester business park and trying to find an outfit I felt semi comfortable in. I was twenty-five and wearing a suit felt like playing dress up.

The day finally came around. I stood dressed in a suit, looking at myself in the mirror. Every route to a job had ended in a nightmare. However, as J.K. Rowling said, 'to not try is to fail by default'. I had to at least try.

On the way to the interview, with Steve driving, we crossed over a roundabout and saw lakes stretching across the left-hand side of the road. There was a fish statue in the middle.

'Fish!' I exclaimed. 'Turn left.' The directions we had said to turn left when we saw the fish in the lake.

We pulled into a quiet car park and the panic coursing through my veins started to peak. Doors. Which door? How do I get through it? What is the other side? Where would I go?

I clutched my folder and concentrated on steadying my breathing.

'I reckon it's that door there. Nowhere says Amadeo though. I'll ask that man,' Steve said.

Oh no. He was always one for just asking people.

He got back in the car and said, 'we are in the wrong place.'

My heart started thumping. I looked at the dash on the car: 9:36 a.m. I was supposed to be there by 9:45 a.m.

He pulled the car out of the car park and turned right, away from the fish and further down the road. We must have turned off too early after we saw the fish. The road kept going, over a little roundabout and we then saw a huge car park straight ahead and a smaller one on the right. As we turned into the small car park we were met by a vast and looming building.

As Steve pulled up, I noticed a suited man walk up to the doors, which opened automatically. Oh, thank goodness, that was one less thing to worry about.

My breath caught as I realised Steve was waiting for me to get out of the car. I was about to walk into a huge investment bank and interview for a role. Twice.

Back to back.

I held onto my folder and walked through the automatic doors. I was met by a row of turnstile things, like the ones you walk through to get onto a train station.

There was a reception desk on the right, where a man sat slouched, looking rather sick of his job.

I approached and said 'Roseanne Weldon, for a job interview.'

'Who with?'

'Oh. Umm.' I hastily opened my folder and looked for the interview invitation. 'Umm, it's two. The first is with David and then it's a … a Jake,' I said, stumbling on my words.

He started shuffling papers around and then picked up what looked like a bus pass. Handing it to me he said, 'take this. If you take a seat over there, I will let them know you are here.'

I sat and watched as people walked up to the turnstiles, put their pass on the top, waited for it to go green and then it would open and allow them to walk through. I tried to memorise their actions so I could mimic them when my time came to face the barrier.

'Roseanne?' a voice called.

I startled and looked around. A man with mousey blond hair that was softly styled had approached me.

'Yes?' I replied.

'Do you want to follow me this way and we can get started?'

No. I did not want to. I wanted to go home. I wanted to sit and play Grand Theft Auto V, not play fancy suit dress up at a bank big enough for scary barriers.

I aced the barrier test and followed him down the corridor, through the doors and down another corridor. I hoped he wouldn't expect me to find my own way out, otherwise I'd end up lost inside the Bank, not a great way to make a first impression.

He opened a side door and held it open for me to walk through.

My eyes darted around the room. Posters lined the walls, the typical corporate stuff. A long table stretched the middle of the room, surrounded by fancy board room chairs. I could see the car park through the window at the end of the table.

A man was already sat at the table. I hadn't noticed him.

I forced a smile and shook his hand, careful not to wipe the contact away afterwards.

Once the interview started, I settled into the back and forth of questions. Interviews were easier than normal conversations. They fired questions at me, either about myself or about the financial theory I had learned, and I answered. It had structure and next to no small talk. I didn't have to ask questions back and the flow of the interview was under their control.

After finishing the second interview, the second set of two men stood to end it. I fumbled my paperwork back into the folder as I stood and navigated the chair and shaking their hands.

I followed Jack back to the barriers, which he had thankfully walked me back to. We approached the barrier and I put my pass on the scanner. As it turned green, I realised he had his hand out to shake. I froze in panic. Was I was supposed to shake his hand again?

He laughed. 'Let's get you through first.' And with that he also scanned his card.

Now safely on the escape side of the barrier I shook his hand and thanked him.

I walked out of the double doors and looked up to the sky. I had done it. I had actually done it. A grin escaped and I made my way back to the car park, where Steve would be waiting for me.

That afternoon's run felt different. I was fuelled by purpose and driven by determination. I had seen a glimpse of the life I wanted. The suits. The swipe pass entry. The stream of office bound workers.

With every beat of my feet onto the belt I rose to the challenge. I set my mind and my heart on working for the Bank of America as a product control analyst, an accountant for traders.

The following day I received another interview invitation from the Bank of America. It was with another two sets of people for the same job, but different teams. I wasn't sure what that meant for how the first two interviews had gone.

I continued on the Bank rat race and attended the

second set of interviews. I had scrambled to find a different suit and that time was led to a room upstairs. At the end of the second interview I was asked if I would like to be interviewed by the vice president, as he would like to meet me.

No, I didn't want to meet someone as important as the vice president of the Bank.

I, of course, agreed to meet him.

The next day I went in and was guided by the original David to, yet another, separate area of the Bank building, to be interviewed, by teleconference, with a vice president of the Bank.

The vice president was on a screen on the wall, David and I sat on the other side of a desk. His voice came out of a speaker in front of us, on a slight delay to the screen.

I gripped my hands tightly as David did the introductions. The vice president then addressed me.

I stared back. I hadn't caught what he said.

My heartbeat thumped as I began to panic.

'These things are a bit tricky with the screen and speaker. It takes some getting used to,' David said.

I managed to have somewhat of a broken, stumbling conversation with the vice president. It was less interview and more informal chat, which did not suit me well.

'I have a meeting at 11 so I need to go now. It was a pleasure meeting you, Roseanne,' the vice president signed off.

The screen went black and I breathed out. I just wanted to go home.

David led me back to the barriers and thanked me for my time for, yet another, interview.

I walked out of the double doors and found Steve waiting for me. That was not fun.

The weeks passed and I enjoyed the June weather. I say enjoyed, I loved watching the blue sky from my bedroom window. It was a three-story house, so I had a view out across the top of smaller buildings.

I passed the time with games and working out, as usual. I decided not to continue submitting job applications until I had my results. Maybe I would do well and that would help tip the scale. I always knew I needed brilliant results to balance my inability to talk to people.

Friday July 7th, I woke up to just another Friday. Without university Friday's didn't mean much. I led in bed and did the usual flick through social media and various apps. Opening Facebook messenger, I sent Craig a Rebecca Black 'Friday' gif. He was always up early, and we had an ongoing joke to celebrate Fridays this way. I smiled as he instantly sent back a dancing duck gif.

Putting my phone down I grabbed the clothes I had laid out the day before and headed to the bathroom.

Half an hour later I was at my desk, ready for the day, drinking my cup of tea. I opened that day's daily jigsaw on the Shockwave website and clicked play on the song I was listening to on repeat, 'Stars' by Skillet.

RING RING!

Oh, come on. I could have at least finished my cup of tea. I looked at my phone and saw Unknown Caller ID lit up across it.

'Hello,' I answered hesitantly.

'Hi, can I speak to Roseanne Weldon please?' the voice asked.

You phoned my phone. It was obviously me.

'Yeah, speaking,' I answered, as I stood up and walked to my bedroom window.

I looked out across the sky, clear skies and still air.

'I am phoning to let you know that the Bank of America would like to offer you the job of Product Control Analyst.'

I stared at a tree ahead.

I had done it?

I had done it!

'Roseanne?' he asked.

Right. You have to reply, Rosie.

'I. Yes. Thank you. That is amazing.'

He went on to outline the salary and the next stages. Not only was the bank offering me a job, but it was enough pay that I could get my own place in Chester and not have to do the big commute each day.

The call ended and I put my phone in my pocket.

I put my palms flat on the windowsill to feel the cold against my skin. I had done it. They wanted me.

I stared at the tree as my mind switched from relief

to all consuming excitement.

My fingers started clicking. My feet started bouncing.

Mum! I had to tell Mum!

I turned and ran out of my bedroom. I bounded down two flights of stairs and slid across the tiles into the kitchen.

Mum stood grinning at me. 'Results?' she asked.

I grinned back. 'No. They offered me the job! The Bank offered me the job!' I practically shouted back.

I started clapping and bouncing as the excitement coursed through me. I celebrated with Mum and then made my way back upstairs to try and vent some of the excitement with music.

I fired off messages to friends and family as I settled back to my puzzle. My feet tapped and my chair spun back and forth as I tried to stay in my seat.

My attention was diverted by an email pop up. 'Your assessment results are now…' was all it showed.

I stopped spinning. My feet settled. Results. Degree results.

I clicked into the email and read the rest, which confirmed that the results were now up on the portal to view.

I clicked Chrome and opened a new tab, then clicked the saved icon and typed in my user ID and password. After what felt like an eternity, the portal page loaded. I clicked assessment and then results. The page loaded. I scrolled past the first and second year results.

I stared at my third year results. 80%, 87%, 84%, 89%, 86% and a trailing tax result of 68%. I expected tax to be low. Other than tax I had smashed it. Tax would get dropped as the lowest module always did.

I opened up my results spreadsheet and keyed in my new results.

My overall degree result was 85%.

A first.

A good first!

I wrote down my results, grabbed the paper and launched of my chair. I sprinted out of my room and bounded down the stairs. I turned into the kitchen and said 'results!'

Mum stood grinning at me. 'What did you get?'

'A first. A good first.' I handed her the bit of paper.

Well, July 7th wasn't a day I was going to forget any time soon.

PUSH THE BUTTON

I stood staring into my own eyes. Mirrors creeped me out.

It was August 22nd. The day had finally come when I would start work at the Bank.

I clenched my jaw and stared at myself.

Steve would take me for the first month because I needed my first pay before the tenancy on my new flat started. At that point, I would have a flat in Chester to move into. It had two bedrooms, one of which I was planning to make into a gym.

I stared at myself. If I wanted that, if I wanted my own flat and my own gym, then I had to get through the day. I took a deep breath and furrowed my brow. I walked out of my room and glanced back. I wouldn't be spending that day at my PC.

My fingers pushed against themselves as Steve pulled up outside the familiar entrance. That time, it wasn't so quiet. There was an almost constant string of people heading through the doors.

I got out of the car and followed the workers

through the doors. It was my first day at an investment bank. Those words, I never thought I'd say.

Once through the doors I became acutely aware of my close proximity to the stream of people. There wasn't much space between the door and barriers, and everyone seemed to fall into rhythm, except for me. I stopped mid-step and tried to regain composure.

I could see the reception. I focused and headed straight to it. I waited behind someone else, who seemed to have forgotten their pass. They were given a temporary replacement and went on their way through the barriers. I looked away from them and back to the reception, to be met by an expectant look. The receptionist looked at me impatiently as I stumbled through explaining it was my first day and I was there to meet Jake.

I took my temporary pass and sat down to wait for this Jake. It was the same seats I had sat on for the interview. I watched as people bustled past and through the barriers. The stream was endless.

I saw a familiar man walking towards me. I really hoped it wasn't Jake as that was the interviewer that I fumbled the handshake and barrier goodbye with. The one that laughed at me. He was very tall and seemed to have a permanent grin, with an almost schoolboy charm about him.

'Hey,' he stopped in front of me. 'You ready?'

Hell no. I was not ready. Maybe I was better off spending the day on my PC after all.

I followed him through the barriers, through doors to the right, then a left turn and straight down a corridor. Two big doors were waiting at the end. He pressed the button to open them and we awkwardly waited for them to come towards us. Why weren't people just pulling the doors open? Why were they all using the button for wheelchair users?

The doors fully opened, and we walked through.

My breath caught as I was hit by the scale of the room. Rows and rows of desks stretched from one wall to the other. Hundreds of people were sat at their desks or milling around. It was like looking at a scene from *The Wolf of Wall Street*. My senses pinged back and forth as I heard typing, talking, clicking, walking, ringing phones, chewing, electric buzzing and I saw screens flashing, feet walking, people smiling, chairs wheeling and the light beaming in through the windows that enclosed the room. My brain whirred while I tried to block it all out. I focused on Jake's shoes and followed him through the maze of desks.

He came to a sudden stop and I almost walked into the back of him.

The people at the desks we had stopped by kept looking at me. I guessed this was the team I would be working with. There was about ten of them and they all seemed young.

I looked back at Jake and saw him pointing to a chair for me. He must have said something. How was I supposed to concentrate on his words, with all the mayhem around us?

I sat down on the chair he was pointing to and moved my hands against each other. I had to find a way to listen.

He started running through my log in details and what I would be doing during my first week. I looked at him as his mouth moved and all the words came out. Luckily, he wrote the log in details down because as fast as my brain was trying to process his words, it was not keeping up.

He then said, 'and this is Zac. It's his accounts you will be training on and taking over.' He gestured to a young guy sat behind us. He must have heard his name, because he turned and smiled at me. He was attractive, for a guy, and clearly worked out, given his stature.

'Hey,' he said, making eye contact with me.

I breathed out and smiled back at him, 'hey.'

I spent the rest of the day watching Zac as he went through the accounts and explained what he was doing. Apparently, he had no problem talking away while I sat quietly and listened. There was so much to take in and I was captivated by it all. My brain was desperate to absorb all the information and do the job justice.

As the day went on, I found it harder to stay awake, let alone focus on what people were saying and manage to respond. At 5 p.m. I was sitting back at my desk doing the mandatory training sessions I had been assigned. They were about things like health and safety and data protection. Thrilling, not.

I was supposed to finish at 5 p.m. But I guessed so was everybody else, yet no one else from the team had left yet. Time ticked on and my mind screamed at me to leave the room. I hadn't taken a lunch. I wouldn't have known how to. I couldn't eat around people and I didn't want to walk away from the room and get lost.

At just gone 6 p.m. a few of the team got up to go. I took this as my cue to grab my bag and head out. I went through the barrier, out the doors and looked up at the sky. I had done my first day at work.

I got into Steve's car and started to apologise for being so late, explaining how I thought they all stayed later than 5pm. Steve, as always, was completely fine. But given how it seemed, I arranged to be picked up at 6 p.m. going forward.

I walked through the front door and into the kitchen. I knew there would be tea waiting for me. I gave Mum a whistle-stop tour of my first day and made my excuses to leave. I just wanted to eat tea at my desk and crawl into bed. Which is exactly what I then did. I sat at my desk to eat my tea and didn't bother turning on my PC. I knew I needed sleep.

I got changed, lined up work clothes for the next day and crawled into bed. I led staring at the ceiling. I had done my first day at work. I was exhausted. It was my first day though, it would get better. I reluctantly set my alarm for 6 a.m. and rolled over to sleep.

The rest of the week went by the same way. I woke up exhausted, I pushed through hours of sensory attacks and I went home exhausted. I was starting to get to grips with the software systems used at work and became comfortable sat with Zac. Some people, for no logical reason, I just feel comfortable with. Thankfully, he was one of those rare people. We would talk of his dedication to fitness and desire to do well in his career.

As the week progressed, I had a horrible realisation. It was all good staying in that one room and not eating, but what would happen in two weeks' time when I was on my period? I had to find a way to use the toilets. First, I had to figure out where the toilets were. I had a tendency to keep my head down and beeline for where I needed to be. I tried to take in my surroundings more and figure out where the toilets were.

By Friday morning I thought I had figured out where they were. It seemed the women's entrance was at the beginning of the long corridor that led to the big room. I took the chance and headed through the door.

I was met by two long rows of cubicle doors. There were over twenty doors down the sides and five sinks on the left-hand side. I walked through the middle and into the last cubicle on the left-hand side. I closed the door behind me and sat on the lid-down toilet. The cubicles weren't tiny. It was so quiet in there. I had just found my favourite place in the Bank.

I left the toilets and carried on down the corridor, towards the main office. I looked at the doors ahead. I really didn't understand why people were being so lazy and not opening the doors themselves. I got to the door and put my hand on the handle. I pulled it towards me. It didn't move. I pulled harder and it slowly made its way towards me. It was so heavy; I couldn't pull it any further. I quickly pressed the disabled button to my left and looked around. Thankfully, no one was watching. I walked to my desk to finish up the day.

Six pm on Friday finally came, I was pretty sure it was going to be my new favourite time. I walked out of the building and looked up to the sky. I had done my first week. I had got through it.

Later that evening, I was sitting with my tea in front of me at my desk, as the PC booted up. I poked the food with my fork and sat in a state of nothing. I forced some of it down and turned my PC back off again.

My phone lit up with Christine's name. We had made plans to play Diablo that night and she must have seen me log back off. I messaged back that I was too tired and was going to go to bed.

'You're going to bed, now? It's 7 p.m. and it's Friday,' she sent back.

'I know. I'm tired,' I replied.

'You're boring,' she sent.

'Piss off, dude,' I sent back.

I had no energy for her crap. I just wanted to sleep.

I set my tablet alarm and crawled into bed, still wearing my trousers and shirt. I was asleep in minutes.

The next morning, I stirred awake and reached across for my phone. The bright light blinded me as I blinked to refocus on the time, 11:30 a.m. I hadn't slept that long in years. I must have taken my tablet at 6:30 a.m. and gone back to sleep. Judging by the tablet packet on the floor, I had done it half asleep.

The weekend went by in a blur. I didn't leave the house and I barely spoke to anyone. I sat at my desk, played puzzle games and listened to music. I missed music so much. I listened to it almost permanently before working. To go such long days without listening to music was taking its toll on me. Not only was my brain being bashed by the noises of the office, but it longed for the comfort of music.

The following Friday was what they called 'month-end', which made no sense, because Friday was the 1st of September. What they meant was, because each day we ran the accounts for the previous day's trading, on the 1st of September we would run accounts for the last day of August. I had no clue what this month-end thing was about, but I had picked up on enough stress and worry to know it wasn't a good thing.

I went through the motions of the week with a wary eye on the looming Friday. When the day arrived, I told Steve that I would text him when I needed picking up, as I had a feeling it would be later than usual.

I walked through the double doors and was met by the noise and bustle of a packed room. People tended to drip feed in and out of the office as days went on, but it seemed everyone was already in and at their desks that morning.

I made my way to my desk and started to log in.

Jake pulled up a seat next to me.

'Hey, how you doing?' He seemed to genuinely care when he asked this.

'Yeah, okay,' I replied, half honestly. I gripped my hands in my lap.

His eyes darted from my hands to my forced smile.

'Things are a bit different today. It just means we have some things to do that we don't normally do. Do you still have training and things to do?'

'Yeah.'

'It's probably best if you get on with that. Most of us will be too busy to do any training today,' he explained.

My day was calm as I worked my way through more of the training sessions. The atmosphere around me was anything but calm.

There were calls across the team to submit, approve and sign off journals. I could hear them on the phone to traders and the trade control team upstairs, trying to get accounts done early so they could move onto month-end tasks.

At around 4 p.m. Jake made his way back up to me.

He looked stressed but still wore his grin as he approached me.

'Do you want to head off? It's Friday and you've had a long week,' he said. He wasn't wrong. 'Trust me this is the only month-end you will get to go early, so you might as well grab it.'

I agreed and headed out of the office, glad to leave the mayhem behind me. I texted Steve that I was already done, but no rush, and tried to follow the road back out towards the lake. I had managed to untangle my headphones and set them playing as I rounded a corner and saw the lake in front of me. I made my way over to the grass and sat down, put my legs out in front of me and watched the water.

The day had been intense. I felt the pressure in the room, everything was being rushed, all of them desperate to reach this month-end goal post. I opened my phone to look at the calendar. The next month-end was the 2nd of October. That is when we would do September's month-end. I began dreading that day.

STARS

Before I knew it, it was the 22nd of September, and I had the keys to my very own flat in Chester.

My family spent the weekend moving me in and helping me get settled. I walked to the shop around the corner a few times with Mum and Jenson, to build familiarity with the area and that shop, if I ever needed it. The plan was to order food online that didn't go out of date, so I wouldn't need to use the shop.

The second bedroom had been set up as a gym. My own little safe haven, in a world of chaos.

After my family left on Sunday afternoon, I stood in the kitchen area, looking across at the lounge and my desk. My own flat. In Chester city centre, where I worked. I wasn't sure how that had become my life.

I walked out of the lounge door and into the gym on the left. My gym. I had all the equipment from my old bedroom set up. I had a pull up station, various free weights and an inverted ab bench.

I walked up to the pull up bar and reached up to grip the bar. I pulled myself up with ease and held the position at the top. I smiled as I released and jumped back to the floor.

However hard work was, I would have this to come home to.

I woke up to my 6 a.m. alarm the next morning. In my bed, in my own flat.

I turned off the alarm and went through the motions of my brand-new routine. I had to leave by 8 a.m. to get the bus. I had done a practice run on the bus with Mum a couple of weeks ago, so I knew the logistics of it. I had £14 in my coat pocket and was ready to ask for a Chester plus week ticket.

The clock neared 8 a.m., so I shut down my PC and gathered my things. My first day getting myself to work was about to happen. I focused on the music playing in my ears and headed out of the apartment block. I just had to get to the bus stop, I would focus on that part first.

I rounded the corner onto a main street, the one that led to the train station. I focused on the pavement in front of me as the traffic noise built around me. I picked up my pace. I turned yet another corner and saw the train station in front of me. I knew it was opposite the train station, so I was close. I finally saw the stop and went to stand against a wall behind it. I preferred the wall because it gave one safe side, and far less chance of people standing close to me or, God forbid, talking to me.

The bus approached and I took out the money from

my coat pocket. Chester plus weekly ticket. Chester plus weekly ticket. That is all I had to say. I had never asked for a ticket before. Chester plus weekly ticket.

The bus pulled to a stop and I took a step forward, to take my place in line with those waiting.

I stepped onto the bus and said my rehearsed line 'Chester plus weekly ticket please.'

'Sorry, what?' the driver said.

I stared back at him. 'Ch... Chester plus weekly ticket please,' I repeated, in line with my rehearsed script.

'How much is it?'

'Umm… uhh £14,' I answered.

He pressed buttons and held his hand out. I passed him the £14 and waited.

'You can take your ticket,' he said impatiently.

I couldn't see a ticket.

He reached across and pulled the ticket that had come out of the machine. He handed that and a red slip to me.

I took it and scurried down the aisle of seats. I found the perfect seat, two rows back from the priority seats and right behind a bell.

My right thumb pushed against my middle finger knuckle as the bus pulled away. I watched out the window while the bus slowly filled, making its way out of Chester and towards the business park.

It turned left at a big roundabout and onto the business park. It stopped for a few minutes at a stop I recognised from the practice run with Mum. My breathing started to pick up, I was very close to my stop.

The bus pulled away and almost instantly someone pressed the bell. Lots of people started to shuffle out of seats. Once they had got off, the bus was fairly empty.

It pulled away and I saw the stop Mum and I had clocked. This was the one I needed to pass and then I could press the bell. As it passed I pressed the red button and stood up from my seat. I walked towards the front and held onto the bar by the driver. I could see the stop Mum and I had got off at ahead, I willed the driver to stop at it.

The bus slowed down and I shuffled off, turning my head back towards the driver to give the impression I had thanked him, but he hadn't heard. I looked up across the lake and towards the sign 'Bank of America Merrill Lynch.' It was 8:30 a.m. on a Monday morning and I was already exhausted. Well, here went another week.

I got through the week and made it to another weekend. I had two days before my first month-end, which would take place on Monday.

Weekends with my favourite human, Jenson, became my saving grace from the pressure I was under at work.

I got home and started tidying up the flat. It was taking everything I had to get through each day, chores were constantly pushed to the weekend. Once the dishes were washed and clothes put out to dry, I sat down at my PC to do a few admin tasks before Jenson arrived. I had applied for the Chartered Institute of Management Accountant (CIMA) exemptions that I was entitled to, from my degree. It meant I would need to sit one more exam to be officially a part qualified accountant. It would be a huge step to realising my accounting dream.

I loaded up my emails to send the documents when I noticed an email from the University of Chester. It seemed I was unable to let go of the institute as I had enrolled to do my masters just after starting at the Bank. They also wanted some final documents, before I would be enrolled. I would be studying for my masters at the same time as chartering and working full time, the first two felt far easier than the third.

Just as I sent the emails back to both CIMA and the university the door to my flat opened and Jenson burst into my hallway.

'Alright, dude?' I asked.

He walked past me and straight to the sofa.

'Good talk,' I joked and sat next to him.

Brushing his cheek with my finger I asked, 'normal takeaway for tea?'

'Yeah,' he smiled back at me. 'What film?'

I laughed. He had been in the flat two seconds and was planning our Friday night's film and a takeaway. I got up to take Jenson's bag from Steve and see him out.

I walked back into the lounge to find Jenson

browsing through Amazon Prime. He had settled on *Wonder Woman*, which I was only too happy to agree to. I put the order in for our takeaway and settled in beside him. With Jenson's head against my shoulder it was easy to fall into the DC universe and away from thoughts of month-end.

RING!

The doorbell made its usual hideous noise and I jumped up to get the food. I walked to the front door and called back to Jenson, 'pause it.'

We had ordered the same thing we always did. Both of us were autistic and we loved nothing more than falling into a comfortable routine. The next morning, we continued our weekend routine and walked to the comic book shop around the corner. We both enjoyed walking the aisles stacked with thousands of comics, though Jenson always seemed to be the one walking out with one in his hand.

The weekend ended far too quickly, and I found myself staring down the barrel of month-end on a Sunday night. I sat on my bed forcing my thumb into my own knuckle. My legs bounced and my breathing thumped through me. Month-end was the next day. I had been doing well with taking on the trading accounts from Zac. I did the same thing every day and had got into the rhythm of it.

The rhythm that worked every day, except for on this ominous month-end that caused a spike in everyone's stress levels. For one day a month we went off grid. For one day a month there was high pressure and a fast pace.

I stood up and started pacing. My heart pumped anxiety through me as I desperately tried to stay in control. I dropped to the floor and put my head in my hands. I pushed against my temples. I knew I had to find a way to calm down.

I looked at the drawers beside my bed.

No. Not like that.

My breathing got quicker and quicker as I fell back and forth with the pressure of my hands on my head.

I stared at my drawers. I got up and walked over to them. I opened my top drawer and felt for the corner. My fingers met cold metal. I pulled out the section of staples I had left there. I walked back to my bed and rolled up my left sleeve.

My breathing steadied as I focused on my arm.

I held the staples in my right hand and put them to my left arm. I pulled, hard, across my skin. A red line followed where the staples had been. I repeated the motion. Again, and again, harder and harder. Until the safe section of my arm, the part people wouldn't see, was covered in red lines.

I breathed out and focused on the searing pain on my arm. I dropped the staples on the floor, pulled down my sleeve and rolled over to sleep.

BEEP BEEP!

My eyes shot open to the alarm. I snoozed it and rolled over.

Ouch!

I flinched away from the bed and pulled my sleeve back. Red lines worked their way across my arms. Spots of blood smudged between them.

Right. I had done that.

I covered it with my hand and walked to the bathroom. I ran the cold tap and put my arm out under it. Shit! I pulled away as tears ran down my face. The pain was overwhelming. I ran my fingertips over the lines covering a now swollen and red raw arm.

I had done that, and I had to deal with the consequences. I dabbed at my arm with a soft towel and proceeded to get suited up, making sure to wear a dark coloured shirt.

I went through the motions of my morning routine. Cup of tea. Morning Minesweeper game.

I was sitting in a trance when my phone lit up.

'Guess what?' were the words I was met by. Christine was right to it that morning.

'What?' I barely had the energy to respond.

She replied, 'I love you.'

I held the edge of the phone to my forehead as yet more tears escaped.

I wiped them away and replied, 'I love you too, dude.'

Later that morning I walked down the corridor towards the huge office. My heart pounded in my chest and my fingers pushed into themselves.

I sat at my desk and fumbled with my coat and bag.

I turned to my PC and hovered my hands over the keys. My fingers couldn't stop hitting into themselves. I couldn't control them to type in my log in. Thumb into finger, thumb into finger. I clenched my hands into a tight fist and slowly released them, trying to regain control.

'Hey, how are things this morning?' Jake's sudden voice beside me made me jump. I hadn't heard him approach.

I stared at my useless hands. 'Yeah, okay thanks,' I lied. 'Just logging in.'

'Can we grab five minutes?' he asked.

'Yeah, of course,' I got up from my seat.

I followed him through a glass door into a little meeting room. I took a seat on the opposite side of the table and stared at the centre of the table. A black conference phone sat there, with far too many buttons.

'I want you to train on your account's month-end tasks today. If you watch Zac do them and then hopefully you can run them next month as he is also doing his new ones,' he started.

I stared at the phone, it reminded me of the one at Marshall's. I wondered what I was doing at the Bank, why I had thought I could do it.

'Everything okay, Rosie?' he looked concerned.

'Yeah, it's just… month-end,' I replied honestly. 'I guess it's just the change. Autism thing,' I blurted out.

'Autism thing?' he looked at me with a strange sense of curiosity. 'I didn't know.'

'But the… the HR people. You are supposed to know,' I stumbled through my words.

'Let's just get through today. I promise you it's not as bad as what you think. Your morning is the same. Then a few extra tasks later that Zac will do with you and I used to do them so I can step in and help at any point,' he reassured me.

I looked up at into his eyes. If I trusted him, I had to trust it would be okay. And I did trust him.

'Okay, yeah,' I said.

The morning was my usual routine, as Jake had promised. At around 1 p.m. I felt a shift in the atmosphere as people skipped their lunch breaks to get the days accounts signed off, keen to move onto month-end tasks. My accounts had a break in them, a difference that I had found and explained to the trader, but now required him to approve it. I had sent the email, but he was notoriously bad at responding to emails, instead preferring to be phoned. I looked at the clock, I had sent the email at 12:30 p.m., it was now 2:30 p.m. I refreshed my emails to find nothing new. I could feel the panic building in me.

I stood abruptly, locked my screen and walked out of the office.

I closed the bathroom door behind me and slid down the wall, bringing my knees to my chest. I took my glasses off and placed them on the toilet lid. My shoulders jolted as I suddenly started crying, the days pressure crashing through me.

Zac was waiting for me to say the accounts were done. I needed the trader to respond but I couldn't phone him. I couldn't ask people to phone him because they were busy with their own stuff. They shouldn't have to help me because I was too messed up to do it myself. I was constantly putting crap on the team and couldn't just do anything myself.

I clenched my fist and hit it repeatedly into my own head. I didn't deserve my job.

But it was my job. Was I going to walk away from it? No. I wasn't.

I got up, put my glasses on and sat on the toilet lid. I took headphones from my pocket and played the song that could always calm me: 'Stars' by Skillet. Opening my phone, I scrolled to that morning's conversation with Christine. I stared at the words 'I love you' as the song played.

As the song ended, I stood up and breathed deeply. Putting my phone and headphones away I left the cubicle and went back to my desk.

An instant message popped up from Jake that read 'how's things going? Accounts done?'

I typed back that I had sent the explanation of the break to the trader and was waiting for confirmation, but he hadn't replied to the email.

Within minutes Jake had walked over to sit next to me. He picked up the phone on my desk and dialled the trader's number. A few moments later he had the response that the trader was fine with the break but hadn't got around to replying to the email.

Jake smiled at me as he said, 'all good?'

'Yeah, all good, thanks.'

It was so simple for him to do what I couldn't. I was a useless part of the team and I just wanted to go home.

Instead of getting to go home, I spent the afternoon watching Zac do the elusive month-end tasks and frantically tried to take it all in, so I could do it in a month's time. He whizzed between spreadsheets, called out to people to approve, pinged out emails and eventually got to the last task. By this point it was 6 p.m. and I was barely able to stay awake.

The next task had a problem and he needed to wait for Jake's help with it. I went back to my desk and watched the time tick away as my eyelids got heavier. At half seven Jake came over to sit next to me.

'Why don't you get on home? I can explain the fix tomorrow. You don't need to stay.'

'Okay yeah, thanks.' I didn't need telling twice.

I walked out of the Bank's doors and tears silently rolled down my face. I put in my headphones and walked to the bus stop. I clenched my fists as I boarded the bus and got beat unrelentingly by the noise and movement on the bus. I got off the bus as tears continued to roll down my cheeks.

When I walked through my door, I dropped my coat and bag where I stood. I turned and locked the door. Still in my suit I climbed into bed, set my alarms, rolled over and stared at the wall.

I wondered if it was all worth it as I fell into a deep sleep.

BEEP BEEP!

My eyes opened to my alarm. I sighed and got out of bed. Great, another day. My legs were heavy, and my mind was empty.

A bus ride later and I was sitting at my desk to face another day.

Jake got up and made a bee-line towards me. I really wasn't in the mood to figure out talking.

'Quick catch up?' he asked.

I nodded and got up to follow him into the meeting room.

He put some documents on the table in front of us.

'So, I went home last night and researched autism. To be honest I didn't really know much about it, but I want to help,' he began to say. 'But, although I've done research, I would rather just talk to you about how things are for you and how I can help you.'

I stared at him in shock. He had really gone to all that effort, for me? My eyes pinged around the room as I fought the urge to cry.

'How are things going, Rosie?' his face was full of concern.

Well that did it. Tears started to roll down my cheek.

'Not great,' I answered, honestly. 'I'm struggling.'

'Okay. So, I will make an appointment with the

occupational nurse here at the Bank for you to see. Then going forward I think we should put some things in place to support you. I'm not sure what yet but between us and the nurse we will figure it out. I'll put into place whatever you need.'

I stared into his eyes. Why was he being so nice? I was nothing to the team. I was the useless team member that couldn't pick up a phone or talk to them.

As if reading my mind, he said, 'Rosie, everyone here needs help sometimes. It might be in different ways and I'm going to be honest and say I have never managed someone with your needs. But that doesn't make it any different that I will support my team however they need.'

The tears came much harder as the emotion of the conversation hit me. I nodded and tried to smile at him.

'Do you want to go home?' he asked.

'No,' I immediately replied. 'I'll be fine.'

'Okay. Go and take a walk and take a minute. I'll talk to the occupational health people and get back to you, okay?'

I did what Jake had advised and went to my hideout - the end cubicle in the toilets. I sat with my headphones in and stared at the back of the door. So, he was going to try and get me help. Help, I always needed help. I needed help at university. I always needed help. I was useless by myself.

I got back to my desk to an appointment invite from an occupational nurse. It was for half an hour's time.

Five minutes before my appointment I got up from my desk to make my way to the room specified in the email. The room was just outside the doors to the office; I had seen others going in and out of there. I stood outside and waited, someone would come and get me, right? I didn't need to knock the door.

The door opened and a middle-aged woman smiled at me. She was dressed smartly and didn't look like a nurse.

'Roseanne?'

I nodded and walked into the room. It was very small. I pushed my chair back away from her as I sat down.

'How are things?' she asked, warmly. Her eyes kinder than I had first thought. Noticing I wasn't going to respond as I stared at her, she continued, 'I'm a doctor here at the Bank.'

Oh, a doctor, that made more sense.

She asked me some basic health questions and probed into my life outside of the Bank.

'I don't do anything outside of the Bank. I go home and sleep. I sleep all weekend. I don't see family much because I'm always tired. I argue with friends because I'm always tired,' I blurted out. If she was going to keep pushing, then she could just know everything. 'I'm just tired,' I finished, caving to the emotion as I started to cry.

'Roseanne, I am going to sign you off work for two

weeks.'

'What? No! I'm fine,' I said as my crying built in intensity. 'I don't want to be signed off.'

She looked at me intently and said, 'this isn't a failure. This isn't stopping working. I think you need to have some time off to rest. Then in two weeks come back and we will do things better. We can work with Jake to make sure things are in place.'

I stared at the floor. I had messed up and now they were sending me away.

'Do you want me to go and get your things for you?' she asked.

'No, I… Can't I finish today? Please, I don't want to let my team down by suddenly going.'

'Okay,' she nodded. 'You should go when your day's tasks are done then.'

I walked out of the room and back to my desk. Before I could start to process what had just happened, Jake appeared next to me.

'Everything okay?' he asked.

'They are signing me off. For two weeks,' I stared at my hands.

Jake didn't miss a beat with how I was coping with it. 'That's okay, Rosie. You need a break. When you come back, we will figure things out, I promise.'

'Yeah.' I had nothing left to say. I just had nothing left.

'Don't worry about finishing today. I don't have much on, I'll do your accounts. Head home and rest up.'

'Yeah,' I repeated. 'Okay, thanks.'

The two weeks went by in a blur. I slept days and nights. I stared at walls and toyed with staples. I went from crying hysterically to feeling nothing for days. I didn't care about family or friends. I had refused to have Jenson as I couldn't face looking at him and feeling nothing. I couldn't face him seeing me like that. Christine's texts had turned into faceless words and my brother's words into a shadow of the man I knew. None of it meant anything.

The Thursday of the second week I opened my phone to mindlessly scroll through social media. My heart lurched I realised what I was looking at. The family Christmas tree on my sister's Instagram. They had decorated the tree without me. I had decorated the tree with them every year. We would play Christmas music and decorate the house and tree. They had done it without me. I was so useless and such a burden to everyone that they didn't even want me there anymore.

I got up and walked to the medicine cabinet. I got out my packs of panic attack tablets and went back to my desk. This time wasn't like before. It felt cold, calculated. I knew the logical answer to the problems was to just stop everything. I would be saving my family from my crap. I would be saving the Bank from my crap. I would be saving myself.

I turned the pack of tablets over in my hands. There was one person I wouldn't be saving. One person whose life would forever be impacted by losing me: Jenson. His rabbit had just died, and he was struggling with the concept of death.

I stared at the tablets. I couldn't do it. Yet again.

I thought back to the letter I gave to Mum when I came out. I had known it was either end my life or find a way to be okay with being gay. Accept defeat, or fight.

I looked at the tablets. If I wasn't going to give up and end it, then I only had one choice. I had to fight like hell.

I stood up as determination rushed through me. I would fight like hell for my life.

ON A BREAK

I walked back into the Bank the following Monday with resolute determination. I would fight, and beat, whatever the Bank could throw at me. I had a meeting with Jake first thing to put a plan into place. Yet again I had fallen and then realised I needed to accommodate my needs.

I walked into the room and smiled as he sat down opposite me.

'You look a lot better,' he said.

'Yeah, I feel a lot better.'

He then proceeded to run through his ideas for adjustments. They included wearing headphones in the office and having a set lunch time. He would go through my processes and try to get me as many routine ones as possible, so that my day was structured. He would also work with me during the month to break down month end and lower the anxiety I was having over it. Upon me saying the times changing every day on the buses and them being busy were difficult he also arranged for me to start at 7:30

a.m. and finish at 4 p.m. every day.

Jake wanted me to email him every day I got in with a number for how I was doing that day, between 1 and 10, 1 being dreadful and 10 being great. This would allow him to know where my head was at that day and how I was coping. I would also see the occupational nurse every two weeks to check in with how things were going.

I walked out of the meeting feeling like, for the first time, I had a fighting chance at holding down the job. I knew it would be the fight of my life to hold down a full-time job but fight I would.

Over the next few weeks I fell into the motions of my adjusted workday. I was now able to go home and work out before eating and going to sleep. I was still exhausted, but it was manageable, I was winning. I had even got through an office desk move. The team had been moved to the other side of the office and I was sitting next to Jake.

It was handy, sitting by the team manager, for things like team meetings. I got up when he did and followed him into the meeting room. I sat down next to Zac, going careful not to sit next to the new person in the team.

'Let's go around the team and do a quick introduction for Stuart,' Jake said, looking around the team. 'I'll start.'

I tried to keep my hands from pushing into themselves. It was Case Study all over again, it would eventually snake around to me. There were four people between Jake and I.

'So, I'm Jake. I've been the team leader for around four years now,' he looked across at me. 'And Roseanne has been here about three months and came from Chester Uni. Okay, now the rest of you.'

I stared at him in shock. He had done my introduction for me. He knew how much distress it would have put me in. I was safe with him.

The introductions carried on around the room. No one seemed to have paid much attention to mine being done for me.

We were dismissed from the meeting and set back to work. I sat down to start my day's work. I logged into the sub ledger system and an error message popped up.

'Eugh, the sub ledger is down,' came Jake's words from beside me. Turning to me he added, 'just do anything that doesn't need it and then we'll just have to wait it out.'

But I saved down the sub ledger data sets first. That was the first step in producing my accounts. I needed to save down the new trial balance, the new positions of the trading accounts. I could feel the frustration building in me. My fingers pushed in against themselves. I needed to start my day the right way. I needed to save the trial balances down.

I stared at my hands. I tried to think what tasks didn't use the sub ledger. They were all part of a puzzle that slowly pieced together throughout the day. Picking out something later in the process was wrong. It should be done later. I decided to wait until the sub ledger was back running and then do it properly, from the beginning. I figured it wouldn't be down for long, the whole business needed to use it.

An hour later, Gregg checked in. 'Sub ledger back?' he asked.

'No, not yet.'

'Have you done anything that can be done without it?' he asked.

'I didn't think it would be down for long,' I answered. 'I would just start from the beginning when it came back.'

He shook his head. 'It could be down for hours. You definitely need to do anything you can without it. Then circle back when it's up.'

He spoke like it made sense to pick apart a routine I had done in the same order every day for months and do it a different way. I did it the first way because it was the best way, the most efficient way. Doing them out of order could cause errors, it would be inefficient.

He left me little choice. I would have to do some of the afternoon tasks.

I opened up the spreadsheet I wouldn't normally until after lunch. That I hadn't ever opened until my accounts were signed off. That didn't lead into my accounts. That shouldn't be done at that time.

I worked through the process as my mind screamed

at me to stop. That I was doing it wrong, it was all wrong.

It felt like pushing against the stream. Like I was forcing something to go against its natural grain. It was uncomfortable, uneasy.

The tasks were finally done, and I sat back in my chair. There were no more tasks that didn't need the sub ledger software. I would have to sit and wait it out like Jake had advised.

A couple of hours later the sub ledger was back up. Mid-afternoon I was starting my day's accounts. Doing what should have been done first thing in the morning. I felt behind, like I hadn't kept up that day with the expected completion times.

I was glad to reach the end of the day and sign off my accounts. It didn't feel like a completed day because it was all so broken. But it had all been done and I could go home. I would go home, sleep and restart afresh the next day. Hopefully, with a functioning sub ledger software from the beginning.

I got through the Christmas period, forced smiles at family members and superficially joined in with the season of joy. I wasn't unhappy, I was just focused wholeheartedly on keeping it together and winning at my career. My career was my purpose and my mind had become consumed by it. I didn't have the energy or the courage to lower my guard and enjoy Christmas. I just wanted to get through it and get to December's month-end. I would beat month-end.

I was sitting at my desk the day before month-end when -

RING RING RING RING

A fire alarm. I looked around to see people standing up. I grabbed my coat and tried to put it on quickly. The ringing of the fire alarm blared through my skull. My eyes desperately tried to focus. The room started to spin. I couldn't find a familiar face. The crowd was jostling, the faces didn't make any sense. No one was at their seats and I didn't recognise any faces around me.

I let myself be moved by the crowd which made its way to a door the other side of the room. People were touching me from every angle. I tried to wipe off the contact, but the more I reacted, the more I felt contact. I put my hands in my pockets, stared at the floor and tried to follow the flow of people.

We broke out of the door and the fire alarm noise eased off. I breathed out. My hands tapped against the inside of my pockets. My feet started to rock onto their sides.

A few minutes later, we were given the all clear to head back in. I had lost my team, so I stuck with the crowd as we went back through the same door we had left through. We got into the office and everyone dispersed off to where they needed to be. I froze. I didn't recognise anything. Was it even the same room? Where was my desk? I couldn't get a grasp of my bearings from this door.

Thankfully, I noticed the main entrance over on the far side. I would go out and then re-enter, so I knew where I was.

I exited the room and decided to have a quick calm down in the toilets first. I entered my cubicle on the end and took my stance on the toilet lid, glasses on the floor in front of me. I let the sensory overload from the fire alarm wash through me and cried it out. I had got better since those two weeks off at breaking in the toilets and then re-building myself. It worked as a release and allowed me to continue with my day. I had become accustomed to the process of crying it out, clearing my face, putting headphones in and refocusing. I took a deep breath and walked out of the cubicle to face the rest of the day. I had beat the fire alarm and I would beat the rest of my day and be ready for month-end the next day.

I went home exhausted but feeling accomplished. Nothing could take the job from me. I worked out for over an hour that night. I increased weights and upped rep counts as determination raged through me. Pain seared through my muscles, but I pushed them harder. I barely slept that night, with month-end looming over me. But I didn't break, and I didn't self-harm.

I woke up and went about my usual morning routine, minus the cup of tea because I felt sick.

By 3 p.m. I had my accounts signed off and was doing the first month-end task. My leg bounced erratically while I willed myself to remember how to do it. Glancing from the process notes to the spreadsheet I started to piece it together. I found the email Zac had sent last month and edited it for this month. One month-end task done!

A couple of hours later I was still stuck on the second task. I needed to ask Zac for help, but he was busy, and I wasn't sure how to turn around and ask him. I couldn't email him because he was right behind me and that would be weird.

'Everything okay?' Jake asked, leaning over. 'You've been staring at that screen a while,' he said, smiling.

I smiled back at him and replied, 'I'm not sure what to do next with this journal.'

He rolled his chair closer and took in the task on my screen.

'Andy can help with that one,' he turned to look over me and called Andy over. Andy walked over and went through the rest of the journal. Two month-end tasks done, one to go.

It was 7 p.m. and I sat working through the last steps of the final journal my accounts needed. Jake turned to me and asked, 'you okay? Do you need to go?'

I grinned at him, 'Nah, I'm good.' I was determined to see this month-end through until the end.

An hour later and I had done just that. My accounts were signed off and all three month-end journals posted.

I walked out of the office with a huge sense of pride and accomplishment. I had done what everyone else had, I had done my month-end accounts.

I wasn't in work the following Monday as I had my graduation to attend. Much to Mum's disappointment, I would not be wearing the cap and gown, neither would I go up the front. I had got spectator tickets for Mum and I; we would sit and watch the ceremony. I wanted to still feel like part of the day.

We set off from my flat because it was just down the road.

'Let's go along the city walls, it will be quicker,' Mum said.

'Yeah, but will it though?' I questioned her. 'We both know how your shortcuts go.'

'Funny. Yes, I'm sure.'

So, we walked along the walls and found ourselves 40 feet up, with no apparent way down.

'Mum.'

'Mhmm,' she tried not to laugh.

We had to double back and find a way down before we could head to the cathedral, where the ceremony would take place. Shortcuts weren't exactly Mum's strongest skill set.

Finally, we made it into the cathedral. For someone who had lived in Chester for four years, I had never been inside the cathedral and was blown away by its beauty.

We found our seats amongst the spectators. I could

see all the students sat further in front. They were talking excitedly amongst themselves. A big day for them. For me, I reminded myself. It was my graduation too.

The business degrees started, and I could see the group making their way down the centre aisle. They had to make their way past me before circling back and walking up on stage. Sarah and Marta smiled at me as they went by. No Christine, standard. I longed to walk behind them. To be a part of one of the biggest days of my life. But there I was, watching, a literal spectator at my own graduation.

After the ceremony Mum and I stood outside while other students gathered into friendship groups.

'Rosie?' Sarah had appeared to my left. 'Come and be in the photos.'

'I can't,' I gestured to my suit.

'Oh, who cares. You are still one of us,' she pulled me along with her. 'I heard about the Bank, sounds amazing!'

I looked at the floor. I wasn't sure she would think it was so amazing if she knew what it was taking me to hold down the job.

We made our way up some stairs outside an old-fashioned building and posed for photos. They were all in gowns and hats, I was not. I wondered how many people below wondered why I was crashing the photos.

I made my excuses to Sarah and went to find Mum.

It didn't feel like my graduation, I wanted to go home. I found her and we headed back to my flat, that time, not via the city walls.

I put my key into the flat door and turned it. I pushed it open and -

BANG!

I jumped and then realised what was in front of me, Jenson stood grinning while party popper flew everywhere around us.

I looked around at my flat. There were balloons and banners on the walls, cakes and drinks on the worktop. I turned to Mum.

'Happy Graduation, Rose. We are so proud.'

I wiped at my eye and grinned. After everything I had put my family through the past couple of months, they were still my people.

We went out that night to celebrate. The university may have failed to make it feel like my graduation, but my family had gone all out to make it feel like a special day.

A couple of days after defeating my first month-end, and then graduation, Jake asked for a quick catch up. I got up and followed him into the meeting room. Meetings with him were no longer bound by anxiety, I was comfortable with him. I trusted him.

'How's things going?' he asked.

'Yeah, great,' I answered honestly. 'Things are going really well at the moment.'

'I noticed some sevens creeping into the score,

that's amazing, Rosie,' he said.

I grinned back at him. For the first time I was content at work. It was taking a lot from me, I was exhausted, but I was happy.

'I asked to talk to you because I wanted to tell you before the rest of the team. I have handed my notice in. I am leaving the bank,' he said.

My heartbeat caught as the ground beneath my feet got pulled out. No. He can't leave.

I stared back at him as a tear ran down my face.

'I… okay,' I said. What else was there to say?

His own eyes swam with tears as he locked eyes with mine.

'I promise you that I will put everything in place for you before I go. I won't let this affect you,' he stated.

'I need you,' I said, perhaps too honestly.

'You don't need me, you never have. You have done all this yourself. And I will make sure you are able to keep doing it,' he said.

January 11th. The day I had feared had finally come. I was saying goodbye to Jake. I wanted to beg him not to leave, to tell him how scared I was to be without him. Finding my feet at the bank had been built around my trust in him. I didn't know if I could do it without him.

I watched him leave and knew one thing was for sure — without Jake there to know when I needed help, I would have to fight harder. I would have to find a way to rise to what others could do. Jake believed in me, and I would not let him down by losing my job.

Without Jake there as my support system I leaned more on Zac. I had felt safe with him from the moment I met him on the first day. He wasn't a manager, so he didn't give me the same protection that my trust in Jake did. But he did make me feel safe when no one else at the Bank did.

After Jake left, he sat Zac in his seat, beside me. He was a welcome distraction from the intensity of the Bank, talking to him was easy. And that wasn't something I say lightly; as an autistic adult, it almost never happens.

A few days after Jake left Zac walked in a little before his start time - he tended to get in quite early. He put his sports bag on the floor between our desks and put on the desk a clear lunch box, with something in it.

'Is that… Is that popcorn?' I asked him.

'Yeah!' he grinned. 'I made it myself last night!'

Of course, he had.

'Right.' I rolled my eyes at him.

'It is low in calories. Just lightly salted for some flavour,' he explained.

Sounded gross.

'It's delicious,' he added.

He proceeded to open the lunchbox and offer me some.

'No, thanks,' I said, pulling away from the smell.

'Your loss,' he said, throwing a piece up to catch in his mouth.

About an hour later he was still picking at his popcorn, with the odd comment about its level of deliciousness and nutrient value, when -

RING! RING! RING!

The fire alarm started.

My breathing instantly started to pick up its pace as I realised what was about to happen. I clenched my fists and willed myself to make it through the next few minutes. I grabbed my coat threw it on. Standing up I looked around, trying to focus my eyes on what was happening, and block out the drilling of the noise in my head.

I recognised the figure in front of me. It was Zac. He was stood looking at me, waiting for me to walk with him. I breathed a sigh of relief and fell into step beside him. I walked closer to him than I normally would, eager to feel safety over the distress I would feel at a stranger's touch.

Keeping close beside him we made it out through the double doors and into the open air. He stood speaking to some people while I stood beside him. My feet twisted onto their sides and my hands pushed into themselves. Zac looked at me occasionally but didn't talk to me. I got away with just standing beside him.

We were given the all clear to enter back into the room and I remained by Zac's side until we reached our desks. I sat down and stared at my hands. I didn't have control over them. All they wanted to do was push into themselves. I wasn't ready to type. I needed to calm down. More to the point, I needed to tip over the edge, and then calm down.

I got up and went to the bathroom, to my own little quiet place. I sat on the closed lid and let the sensory overload come out. The tears fell as I sat clenching and unclenching my fists.

Once I could feel it easing off, I put one headphone in and played 'Stars.' The ticking as the song started was enough for me to fall into my safe bubble and helped restore my composure.

The song finished and I took the headphone out. Standing up I stared at the back of the cubicle door. I needed to get through the day, then I could go home to eat and sleep.

I made my way back into the main office, pushing the button to enter, yep, I had learned that lesson.

I sat down at my desk and spread my fingers over the keyboard, focusing on controlling them. I could feel the aftereffects of the sensory overload, but it was better after letting it run its course in the bathroom.

'You okay?' Zac asked, turning to look at me. He looked from my puffy red eyes to my hands, static above the keyboard.

'Yeah,' I started to lie but noticed the concern on his face. Genuine care was etched in his frown. 'Fire alarms are hard, gonna be a tough day,' I added.

'I know,' he smiled. 'But you did it. You got

through it. I say we choose to try and move on and enjoy the rest of the day. I for one am going to enjoy it with my delicious popcorn. Maybe you need some, to improve your day.'

I laughed at him as he grabbed another handful out of his almost empty lunch box.

After Jake left, my hours crept up and my lunch breaks became less frequent as I drilled through everything the Bank threw at me. I walked out of the office one evening at 7 p.m. Having started at 7:30 a.m. I was exhausted. Feeling exhausted had become my new normal. Breaking into pieces in the bathrooms multiple times a day had become the new normal. Attending conference meetings with New York, minutes after panic attacks, had become the new normal. But I was working full time as an investment banker. I was so proud of what I was achieving.

I was sitting on the bus a week after Jake left when my watch buzzed. It would be Christine. I was so focused on the Bank, so focused on surviving each day, I knew I was being a bitch to her.

'We need a break,' the message read.

A break? We weren't in a relationship; how could we have a break? I knew what she meant. We burned so intensely that we often had cool off periods where we needed time apart. But I didn't want a break. I needed her.

'I don't want a break,' I replied.

After sending the message, realisation hit me. She

didn't deserve the backlash of me holding down my job. I hadn't meant to treat her that way, she was so close it just kind of happened. I didn't have the energy to care about her. It was as simple as that.

'Okay, yeah. I agree, let's have a break,' I sent.

I sat at my desk that day looking out the window. Snow started to fall. It was snowing! I loved watching the snow. Christine loved the snow. I pulled my phone out. No, we were on a break. I put it away and watched the snow fall, I hoped she was watching it too.

My watch buzzed so I pulled my phone out.

'Breaks over, it's snowing!' Christine's message read.

I grinned into the message. What an idiot. An idiot I loved dearly. I had to get my shit together and stop moaning to her about work stress.

February the 1st 2018 was my biggest test to date. A month-end, without Jake. I was no longer a new employee. I was supposed to be able to handle it. I went to bed on January the 31st raging with determination. Nothing would prevent me from making it through month-end the next day, I would do whatever it took.

The next morning my heart pounded, and my fingers gripped against each other as I braced myself for the day ahead. I walked towards my desk with purpose and logged in to start my day. My legs bounced and fingers flicked while I drilled through the noise of the office and worked through my morning tasks.

By 3 p.m. the clock became my enemy as I raced against time to get my accounts signed off. I still hadn't moved onto the month-end tasks because there was an abnormal break on my accounts that needed to be sorted.

I span back and forth in my chair and stared at the time. I needed my accounts boxed off so I could move on. Everyone else was so busy that no one had noticed my accounts weren't done. Did I go to my new manager? I looked over at him. He looked busy, stressed.

I got up and walked to the toilets. I sat down on the lid and clenched my fist. I lifted them and forcefully punched them down into my thighs. The dull thud of pain hit me as I tried to focus. I needed to tell someone that my accounts weren't done yet.

My watch buzzed against my wrist. I opened my phone to see Christine's name and the message 'how's dooms-day going?'

I knew she was joking, but it was far from funny.

I typed back 'shit, I feel like an elastic band wound so tight I'm going to break.'

I went on to explain what my situation was, to which she not so helpfully replied 'just tell your manager.'

Easier said than done. Jake would have asked me how it was going by now. Yes, but Jake wasn't there. I had to figure it out for myself.

My legs bounced faster and faster while my heart continued to pound. I bolted up onto my feet and threw my fist against the wall, stopping millimetres before contact. I hadn't got that far to lose.

I unclenched my fists and put my palms against the door in front of me. I concentrated on slowing my breathing down and regaining control. Gritting my teeth, I walked back into the eye of the storm.

I sat at my desk, immediately clicked new email and typed in my manager's name. I typed out that my accounts still weren't signed off yet and I was concerned over the day's time. I clicked send before I had a chance to second guess it.

A few minutes later my manager replied that he had seen the thread of emails and I was doing the right thing. There was nothing to do but wait for the analysis to come back from the trader. My legs bounced while anxiety flowed through me. Okay, I just had to wait it out. I refreshed my emails as I waited for the trader to reply.

At 5 p.m. the trader finally replied, and I got my accounts signed off for the day. I was ready to move onto the month-end accounts. I loaded up the first journal and tried to focus. My hands clenched as my feet bounced. I pushed my nails into my hands to try and clear my mind.

I tried to remember Jake's training on the month-end tasks. They were just journals, I had to work through them as usual. Three hours later and I had done the first two and sent them out for approval. Just one month-end journal to go and I could go home.

My manager had offered for me to bail out, but I could tell he was busy and didn't really want me to leave. I would finish my job.

By nine o clock I was still staring at the third and final journal. There was only me and a couple of others left in the office. My legs bounced rapidly as my breathing picked up. I pushed one palm against the other and willed my eyes to focus on the spreadsheet in front of me. My body was shutting down on me. I put my hands onto my thighs and squeezed against the bruises from earlier. The pain forced my eyes to focus and I was able to drill on with the journal.

At ten o'clock my manager came over to help me approve and submit the final journal. I had done it. Thankfully there was still one bus left to catch before they stopped for the night.

I dragged myself to the bus stop in time to catch it. Every part of me felt like it was made of lead as I dragged myself into my flat and crashed onto my bed. Fully dressed, with no tea, I set my alarms and fell face down on top of the duvet. As I drifted off to sleep, I smiled to myself, I had done it. I hoped Jake would be proud.

FOOTSTEPS

My eyes opened and I stared at the ceiling. A huge grin washed over me. I had done it! I had made it through my first month-end, from start to finish, and done all the tasks myself.

I stood up and realised I was still wearing my suit. I needed to get sorted and ready for work, my grumbling stomach would have to wait. I couldn't help but smile while I walked to the bus. Was I exhausted? Of course. But I had done it. I was doing it.

I got off the bus and made my way through the business park. I kept hearing a strange noise, above my music.

Thud. Thud.

I looked around. What was making that noise? It stopped as I did, I shrugged and continued walking.

Thud. Thud.

I looked down. It was coming from below me. I looked down as I took another few steps.

Thud. Thud.

My right foot was slamming into the floor with

every step. I tried to lower it slowly with the next step.

Thud.

Okay, well that was weird. I was sure it was nothing. I made my way to the Bank, thuds and all.

Later that day I sat on the lid of the toilet to calm down from sensory overload and looked at my right foot. I tried to raise my foot off the floor, but nothing happened. What the hell? I willed it to move so hard my whole leg started shaking uncontrollably. I couldn't lift my foot off the floor.

I opened the door off the bathroom and walked slowly through the middle of the cubicles. My right leg bent at the knee and then flopped my foot forward. My actual foot wasn't moving, it was being propelled forward and then landing on the floor with a thud.

It would be fine. I was exhausted and I hadn't eaten. It was Friday and I would rest at the weekend.

By Monday my foot thud had got worse as I began to lose more control of my right leg. Upon my mum's panic I had agreed to see an out-of-hours doctor after work. I would not take time off work for it when I was finally succeeding at the Bank.

I walked into the doctors with a stiff right knee and a thudding right foot. After a brief examination and a few questions, he decided the muscles had seized up and I needed some tablets to help them relax. I was happy to be given some medication and sent on my way, while being perhaps a bit smug to Mum that it wasn't a big deal.

'I don't think this is okay, Rose. I'm worried about you,' Mum said to me as we got back into the car.

'It's nothing. I'm fine. Work is going amazing,' I automatically said.

'I'm not talking about work. I am talking about you. You are working too hard.' She gave me the look only a mother could.

I shrugged it off and we headed back to my flat.

I did plan to take the medication, but that night changed things. It became clear that what was happening with my legs, was more than it had first seemed.

I led in bed and began getting strange sensations in my right foot. Tingling feelings began snaking up my leg as they intertwined with sharp twangs of pain. My legs felt like a matrix of red-hot wires being randomly twanged against its insides. I sat up and looked at my leg. It looked fine.

I tossed and turned all night as the pains went up and down my leg, building in intensity. Okay, I would give it to Mum, something was not right.

A week later I was sitting opposite a neurologist. Working for the Bank came with private medical care which meant I could jump the NHS queue and see someone pretty rapidly. He asked me questions about my leg and general health, which by this point was not great. I had become weak and tired as I increasingly dragged my right leg around that refused to work for me. He also asked questions about my mum's health, focusing in on her sarcoidosis and suspected Multiple Sclerosis (MS) when she was younger.

'I think we should do a nerve conduction test to look for nerve damage and also an MRI of your brain and spine,' he said.

'I... okay. What is the MRI looking for?' I asked, not knowing if I wanted the answer.

'Multiple Sclerosis,' he stated nonchalantly.

'Right. Of course, it is.'

I went home and googled MS. I googled if you could work with MS. Could I make it work? Fight this MS thing and still work at the Bank?

A week later and it was time for this nerve conduction test.

'Take off your trousers, shoes and socks and get onto the bed,' the doctor asked.

I did as he said, feeling exposed as I tried to climb up onto the bed. My right leg kept giving way as I tried to climb up. I gripped the bed with my arms and heaved myself up and over, onto the bed.

The doctor walked over to me with a three-inch metal rod in his hand that was attached by a wire to a machine.

'I'm going to put this into your muscles and then ask you to move. I will then use the shocks,' he said.

Into my leg. Shocks. What?

He pushed the rod into the back of my calf muscle. My back arched as my hands gripped the bed. Tears began rolling down my face. I wanted the nightmare over with.

He leaned over to press a button. A shock ripped from the rod through my muscles as my foot twitched uncontrollably.

He proceeded to remove and replace the rod in various muscles on my leg and shock me. At one point he didn't seem to be getting what he wanted, so he twisted the rod in the muscle under my knee. He continued shocking this muscle, clearly looking for something.

He removed the rod and nodded at me. 'Okay, all done, you can get dressed,' he said.

Well thanks, evil electric man.

I wiped off the spots of blood over my leg and tried to get dressed, while balancing on one leg. My right leg shook as it cried out in pain.

'There is damage to the nerve beside your right knee,' he said as he scribbled onto paper.

I stared at him. 'What does that mean? Can that heal?' I hoped for him to say yes.

'Yes, it can, in time. But you will still need to have further tests as it could be part of something else. This damage doesn't explain all your symptoms,' he explained.

All I heard was that there was nerve damage and it could heal. Everything was going to be fine.

A few days later I got myself into bed, now using a crutch. It was impossible to walk without one as my leg constantly gave out and caused me to fall. I was just dragging around a useless leg.

I looked up at the ceiling while the usual pains went up and down my right leg. Was it my new normal? I thought about the nerve damage. It was a good thing they have found something concrete, but I knew as well as that neurologist that there was a lot more to this than a nerve being damaged. That wouldn't explain why I felt so weak and tired, or why the pains and loss of function were still getting worse.

I led there and started to feel tingling in my left foot. No. Please, not the left leg as well.

A spider started crawling up my left leg. I threw the duvet off and looked at my foot. There was nothing there. The sensation continued up my leg and back down. The same matrix of pains I had lived with for a month in my right foot began consuming my left.

Tears started to fall. I fell onto my back and looked at the ceiling. It wasn't fair. What had I done to deserve it?

My right leg started to twitch. A burning feeling built in the sole of my foot. A sudden sharp pain ripped up through my leg to my thigh. My back arched as I silently screamed out. My body convulsed in pain as I prayed for it to stop. My hands gripped the bars behind my head.

The pain stopped. The longest four seconds of my life. I put my arms over my head and cried for the first time since losing my leg. I let the fear wash over me. I was terrified. I wanted my legs back. I wanted the nightmare to be over.

After that night the pain in my right leg had magnified and my left leg joined the party of being useless. Dragging myself around had become the new norm. I was now so restricted that I had to get taxis to and from work.

Using taxis everyday was an interesting experience for someone who is autistic. They liked to talk, a lot. One particular morning I knew the journey was going to be trouble when he asked, 'which way do you normally go, love?'

Firstly, don't call me love, and secondly, wasn't it his job to know how to get there?

'I don't know,' I mumbled back.

'Don't you do this journey every day?' he laughed.

'Yeah.'

I looked away from his laugh and out of the window. I could never grasp directions and places; my mind just didn't absorb them.

The car came to a stop and I opened the door, using my crutch to stand up. I shut the car door and looked around. This wasn't the Bank. That building, that wasn't the Bank.

I turned back to the car.

'I… this —' The car pulled away.

Fear hit me as I looked from my incapable legs to my surroundings. Where was I? From the style of buildings, I was sure I was on the business park somewhere.

I pulled out my phone and text Charlie to explain what had happened.

'Did you see where the taxi went after you got out?' he sent.

I tried to remember. I was stood in a car park. There was a road to my left, but it looked like a dead end. The taxi must have gone to my right.

'I think so,' I replied.

'Follow the way it went. It should take you back to a main road. Then see if you recognise anything.'

Okay. Yeah. That made sense. Except, for one thing. I looked down at my legs and prayed they would keep going until I found the Bank.

I leaned against my crutch and made my way down the road that lead out of the car park. I turned the corner and saw it stretch out a good 90 metres in front of me. A few months ago, that would be a minute's walk. On that day, it was my Mount Everest. I could do it. I put one foot in front of the other and drilled through the pain shooting up my legs, they were screaming at me to stop.

I reached the end and looked up and down a busy road. My heart sank, I knew where I was. I was further along the business park than the Bank. I was a five-minute walk from the Bank, a five-minute walk if I had my old legs.

I got my phone out and called Charlie's number.

'I know where I am. I am a long way from the Bank. With my legs, it's a long way,' I said. Then the determination and strength washed from me as the tears started to fall. 'How am I going to get to work?'

'Phone the taxi again? Phone work?' he started shooting solutions at me.

'I would look stupid. I'm not that far away,' I looked down at my useless legs. 'It's just a long way for me today.'

I said my goodbyes and put the phone away.

This would hurt.

Half an hour later I sat down at my desk. Pain seared through my legs. I put my face in my hands, I couldn't stop crying.

After explaining to Zac what had happened, he asked for my phone. Strange request but I handed it over to him.

A few minutes later he leaned into me and smiled. 'Hey, look.'

He held out my phone with a screen lit up. It was Google Maps.

'I have screen shot this office's location on the map, okay? You show this to the taxi driver. Then you don't need to remember or talk,' he said. 'And if something like this ever happens again. You phone me.'

The day of my MRI came around faster than I would have liked. The thought of being dressed in a gown and put into a restricted tube with loud noises, didn't exactly appeal to me. I stood in the changing room, clenching and unclenching my fist. If I wanted to know what was going on, I had to get through it. My whole body shook as I forced myself to open the door and tell the nurse I was ready.

The gown was hitting against my legs and pulling around my neck. I wore the same clothes every day, I would buy the same jeans or top just in different colours. And there I was, in some weird gown that was brushing against me. I leaned against my crutch and I got myself to the nurse.

'Are you sure you want to do this?' I could read the concern on her face. My physical presentation insinuated a lack of consent.

'Yes. I just want it done,' I said. I shook as I began to cry.

They helped me up onto the bed and strapped my head and legs down. They explained they would inject into my arm halfway through. I stared ahead and willed time to move faster, for it to all be over. They pushed me back into the tube. It arched over my body, barely. The machine churned into action and roared around me. I knew I had to stay still. It would ruin the images if I moved.

I led perfectly still, for an hour. A prisoner in my own body.

That wouldn't be the last test I had for my legs. The process continued with more tests, more scary illnesses being looked for and more results. They found signs for nerve damage and sarcoidosis, they ruled out MS, ALS and a brain tumour. I dragged myself into taxis and to work every day. I worked on a redesign process that took me back to twelve-hour days and high stress conference calls. Even with everything thrown at me, I was still winning, I was still working.

It had got to the point that I had accepted I could no longer work out. I could barely walk and was so weak that any exercise hurt me. I opened the door to my spare bedroom, my gym. I had closed the door a couple of months prior, the sight of it was too painful. I sat in the middle of the room and looked from the home gym machine to the free weights. This was once my happy place, an escape from the outside world. Yet there I sat, crutch led down beside me, barely able to walk.

I pulled myself up using the crutch and took my phone out. I began taking photos of all the equipment. It all needed to go. I had to accept that fitness was not part of my life anymore.

A week later and I stood in the middle of an empty second bedroom. I knew it was for the best. I had to move on.

At work, coming up with Google map suggestions wasn't the only way Zac was supporting my difficulties. He had come up with a plan to help me overcome using the phones. He wanted to use how safe Harry Potter made me feel, to get me into the habit of talking on the phone. He was so excited about his plan; it was impossible not to agree to it.

One afternoon, once the accounts were done, he was keen to put the plan into motion.

'Okay, I'll call you in a couple of minutes.' He

looked at my legs and corrected himself to, 'okay, five minutes.'

I gave him a firm look of 'I don't want to be doing this' and grabbed my crutch to head out.

I stood out the front of the Bank, beside the bike racks, and waited for his call.

His name lit up on my phone. I took a deep breath and answered. I hated talking on the phone. It was purely verbal. There was no alternative but to find something to say, and fast, or face awkward silences.

'Okay. First question,' he said. He was getting right to it. He knew I wouldn't like small talk. 'When did Lily and James die?'

'October 31st, 1981,' I said straight away.

'How could you possibly know that?' I smiled at the shock in his voice.

'They died on Halloween, so that is October 31st. They died when Harry was one. Harry was born July 31st, 1980,' I relaxed against the wall as I explained the logic behind the answer.

'I may need some harder questions,' he said. 'The four marauders?'

'Padfoot, Moony, Wormtail and Prongs,' I answered. Then just for completeness added, 'or, Sirius, Remus, Peter and James.'

'Right,' he said.

I could hear his breathing as I waited for the next question.

'You're looking for harder questions, aren't you?'

'Okay,' he said, sounding pleased with himself. 'What page does Snape ask them to turn to when he covers Lupin's class?'

'How on earth am I supposed to remember that?' I asked, as he laughed down the phone. 'Two hundred and ninety-five?' I guessed.

'Nope, 394.' I could hear the smile in his voice when he added, 'can't believe you call yourself a Harry Potter fan.'

'Mean,' I said.

'So, how's work going today?' he asked.

I froze as I tried to process the question. How was work going that day? I started to think of everything that had happened that day and try to decipher what would be relevant to answer with. Having no clue how much he wanted to know, I settled with, 'yeah, okay.'

'You wanna come back in?' he asked.

'Yeah,' I said, hanging up the call.

I limped back into the office and sat down beside him.

'That was sneaky, throwing in the work question,' I said.

He put his hands up in mock self-defence and smiled. 'Just trying to help.'

He turned to face me and gave me a questioning look. 'So, you wanna do the redesign call later?'

My accounts were undergoing a redesign process. This involved me testing a new process and building spreadsheets around what it needed. I was putting in a huge amount of work, but Zac was feeding it back via daily conference calls with the managers in London. He was doing it to support me, but I knew he wanted me to get more credit for what I was doing, behind the scenes. I would have loved to have fed it all back. I was so proud of the work I was doing. But I couldn't talk on the phone, in a conference call, with managers in London.

Almost as if he had read my thoughts, he added, 'not to talk! Just to listen.' Then he launched further into, 'I have been thinking about it. Why don't you dial in with your mobile? It's something you are comfortable with. You can just wear your headphones and listen to the call. You don't need to talk.'

He wasn't wrong. It was a good idea. Corporate phones terrified me. I would just be wearing my own headphones. I wouldn't need to talk.

'Okay,' I gave in. 'Just to listen.'

He fist pumped the air and turned back to his desk. What a dork.

I did listen in to the call later that day. I felt more involved in the process and could hear them discussing the plans and praising the work I had completed up to that point.

It was good timing for me to feel like I was achieving something at work, because I had a performance review later that afternoon. The boss from London was in Chester to have individual meetings with the whole team. I hadn't been working there long enough for it to be an official performance review, but he still wanted to do it, informally.

I followed him up to the canteen, where we would have the meeting. Of all the settings, it wouldn't have been my first choice. People bustled around as we took out seats at a small table off to the side.

I was keen to keep the conversation away from my health and focused on work. I didn't want my achievements being overshadowed by autism and failing legs.

'The Bank will support you in any way you need. You're doing a great job so far, Roseanne. The redesign is looking really great,' he concluded, standing up to shake my hand.

I made my way back down the stairs, no easy feat with the crutch. But no, even with failing legs, I was not getting in the floating tin box of a lift.

I sat back to my desk and wondered if I had done okay in the performance review. The boss man seemed happy with me. Even with my failing legs, I seemed to be keeping up with everything at work.

'—tomorrow, I think. I think I'm sitting over the other side, by the door.'

Was it me, or did that sound like someone in the team was talking about a desk move?

I got home that night and slept uneasy as I pondered on alternative meanings to those words. Maybe just that one person was moving. Maybe it wasn't a whole team shuffle.

I got in the next day to the news that it was the whole team moving desks. I was going to move a row back. And not be sat next to Zac. Instead I would be next to a different guy in the team. He was okay, but he wasn't Zac. Jake had left, and now they were taking Zac from me.

I sat at my new desk and logged in. The whole room looked different from that seat. I could hear different voices from those around me. I opened the sub ledger software and tried to go about my day. I couldn't focus. Everything felt wrong.

'Everything okay?' Zac appeared stood beside me.

Tears filled my eyes as I answered, 'I guess. I didn't want to be moved from you.'

'I know,' he smiled softly. 'I tried saying to the Chester manager that you wouldn't like it.'

The tears spilled over as I looked at him. I felt so safe with him. I didn't want to sit away from him.

'Let me talk to the London manager,' he said, looking determined.

I wiped at my eyes and tried to focus on my screen. I needed to get some work done.

An hour or so later an instant message popped up from Zac which read, 'I'm going to swap, to sit next to you tomorrow. Just gotta deal without my top banter for a day :)'

I smiled at the message. I just had to get through one day and then Zac would be back beside me.

BANTER LEGEND

Five months after the day of the thudding foot, I had a neurologist appointment. As I walked into the room, he looked at me, concerned. Why was he concerned? Should I be concerned?

I got myself sat down and put my crutch down beside me.

'We have exhausted all physical explanations of what is causing this,' he said, nodding to my legs. Was he going to say they didn't know what it was? Something had taken my legs from me, figure it out and get them back!

'I think it is Functional Neurological Disorder,' he said.

'Okay… what is that? Will it get better?' I asked. I just wanted to walk again.

'It means there is no underlying physical cause. That the symptoms have been driven by psychological causes,' he explained.

Anger built in me. I stared at him and said, 'I am not faking this. I can't use my legs!'

'That is not what this means, Roseanne. Let me explain please,' he said.

He went on to explain that he believed my legs had stopped working because of a break between the psychological connection of body and mind.

'What happened before the symptoms appeared?' he asked.

'I... I was... ' I mumbled as realisation hit me like a ton of bricks. 'It was month-end at work the day before. I... I did it... I won,' I said. Even as I said it I knew I sounded ridiculous.

Won, Rosie? You lost your damn legs because of that 'win.'

'Sometimes our bodies are very clever at finding a way to slow us down,' the doctor explained. 'Even if we don't want to. You need to remove the triggers of what caused this, Roseanne. I will also be putting you through physiotherapy to try and get movement back. But there is no point doing that if you continue to be in the environment that caused it.'

Was he telling me to quit my job?

I got home that evening and researched this Functional Neurological Disorder. I scrolled through endless websites and took in what it was all saying. It was essentially malfunctions in the body, triggered by an event or situation. After the body is altered by the event the disabling symptoms are very real and outside of the persons control. I really couldn't lift my foot or control my leg, because my mind had forgotten how to do it. My mind wasn't registering my legs properly because I had pushed myself so hard psychologically that the connections had snapped.

I stared at my legs. I had done it to myself.

Was this it? I had tried to outsmart the system and use academics to get me a job, which failed. I had tried to work harder and give more, to compensate for my weaknesses and now that had failed. Was my career over? Did I have to face the facts that I couldn't hold down a full-time job? That the 16% of autistics in full-time work wasn't meant to be me.

The next day I went into work and made an appointment with the occupational nurse. I explained everything that the doctor had said and that he advised I should walk away from the Bank. She signed me off work for a month. I would attend physiotherapy, rest up and try to get my legs back. I cried as we agreed that the Bank probably wasn't best for me, but we would come up with a plan upon my return, perhaps a different role within the Bank would have less impact on my health.

I walked out of that meeting and took a pit stop in my favourite Bank place: my toilet. I needed to go and tell my manager that I was being signed off for a month and what the doctor had said. I started to feel guilty about the impact this would have on my team but caught myself. I looked at my legs and tried to control movement, they shook aggressively back at me. No chance.

Was the job more important than my health? Would I pass up running with Jenson so I could work at the Bank? Would I risk my life, for a job? My career had been the purpose consuming me for so long, I didn't know what my new purpose was. Happiness? Health? What was I going to strive for, work towards?

I gathered my thoughts and made my way to the meeting with my managers. I explained what had happened and they sympathised. They weren't annoyed at me being signed off, but relieved I had a chance to get my health back. They explained that your career should never come above your health. Well I had sure as hell learned that lesson the hard way. I saw with crystal clear clarity that my health was the most important thing in my life, and it would not come second to my career again.

I walked, well, half stumbled, half dragged myself, out to the taxi waiting for me. I turned and looked at the Bank. I had given everything to it. I was willing to give everything to it. Never again, Rosie, never again. I turned and ducked into the taxi.

As we pulled away from the Bank my phone lit up. Something had been posted in the old university graduation group. There hadn't been a post in there since a year prior. Something in me wanted to see what it was. I opened the notification and saw a post saying an accounting firm in Chester was looking for graduates to join as accountants. It was set hours, in town, and the tasks were financial accounting based. I couldn't help but feel I was meant to apply.

That night when I got home, I put my crutch by the front door and dragged myself to my desk. I opened my CV and updated it to include the Bank. I sent my CV to the accounting firm. I had nothing to lose.

The next day I woke with a new sense of purpose. To get my legs back. I had been assured by the doctor that I could not do any further damage to my legs. I was given the all clear to push them to get them back. If there was one thing that I was not short of, it was determination. I was a stubborn shit and that was about to come in very useful.

I put on motivational music, yes that play list included 'Eye of the Tiger' and stood on one side of my rug. The rug had various squares and lines on it, I would try to walk within the lines, control my steps.

I focused on my feet, willing myself to control them. I lifted my left foot and placed it onto the first line. I lifted my right foot and pain ripped through my leg and took me to the floor. I got back up. Again, Rosie. I tried again. I fell.

'Aghh!' I cried out and I punched the floor.

I got back up and reset my position. Again, Rosie.

I sang to the music as I stood there. Music, I thought, use music.

I rolled my chair into the middle of the room and put on Andy Black's 'Stay Alive'. A song with brilliant drumming throughout.

The music beat through me as I tried to move my

feet to the music. Frustration built in me because I couldn't hit the beats. I couldn't control my feet enough to stay in time.

You don't need perfection, Rosie, just build up movement and control.

I ignored the existing beat and added layers of my own. I watched my feet move in unpredictable patterns, partly controlled, partly uncontrolled. But it was movement. I smiled at them as the music washed through me.

A new email popped up on my PC. The accounting firm was inviting me to an interview. I was long past going into situations unprepared. I opened Google Maps and looked for where the office was. It was just off the high street; I was familiar with it. I looked at the entrance, it was an intercom.

I pulled out my phone and sent a text to Ashley. After giving her a whistle-stop tour on why I was going for an interview, I asked her for a breakdown of how to use an intercom. She gave me a script of what to say into it and how long to wait before buzzing again.

The interview was in a week. I had to be able to walk into it reasonably normally, so as not to bring attention to my legs. The last thing I needed them to know was why I was leaving the Bank. Having a psychological breakdown and losing the use of my legs, it didn't really shout 'hire me.'

The day of the interview I left my flat for the first

time without crutches. My pace was slow, the pain intense. I put one foot in front of the other and tried not to grimace with pain. Pain shot up and down both legs as I focused with all my mind on walking. I could no longer go on my phone while I walked, I had to focus.

I looked up to take in the beauty of Chester's clock. I thought back to the countless times I had walked under it with Christine. We had walked past the office I was heading to every day. I smiled at the memories, let out a breath and turned the corner that lead to the office. I was in agony. But this interview, this shot at a different job, this was for my legs. I would be completely honest about who I was and what I could do. I would not claim to be anything that I wasn't.

Would any employer really want to hire me? An employee who can't answer phones, can't talk to their team, and has now faced, can't work under intense pressure and long hours. But I had to give it a shot. I had to let my guard down and see where I really stood. Which right then, was stood staring at an intercom. I breathed in and pressed the 'Exchequer' button. I spoke my scripted line and the doors in front of me opened.

I sat in the interview room with two young women opposite me. They seemed nice, friendly. I didn't force eye contact. I told them I was autistic. I told them I didn't do well with phones. In fact, I was so brutally honest I am surprised they didn't just immediately send me out for wasting their time. I skirted around why I was leaving the Bank. I floated through the questions on accounting and finance, my academic past and how dedicated I was to my field. I could talk about that all day.

I said my goodbyes and walked out of the room, willing my legs to hold my weight. I got back outside and ran my hands up and down the lower half of my legs, trying to reset them from the weird feelings. It had become a useful way of recalibrating what they could really feel and what wasn't there. I had put them through a lot, I needed to get home and then I would rest.

For the next few days I fell into a rhythm of sleeping, studying, legs rehab and more sleeping. Towards the end of the week I heard back from one of the women in the interview. The director of the company wanted to talk to me, on the phone. Awesome, brilliant, I loved talking on the phone, especially to important people like directors of companies I was interviewing for, not.

The director explained on the call how she didn't think I was suited for the role I had applied for, that it wouldn't suit someone who couldn't use the phones and talk to people. Okay, thanks. Did she need to phone me to tell me what I had been told my whole life? That I had no value when I couldn't talk to people.

'I would like to interview you, personally, for a different role,' she continued. 'I think we can find something that would be more suited to your skill set.'

I held the phone against my ear and willed my mind to think of a reply. Find something suited to my skill set? A role for exactly who I was? No jumping through hoops, no trying to be what I wasn't. Is that what she was saying?

'This job would however be for a salary of £xx,' she continued.

My heart sank. I should have known there would be a catch, that was significantly lower than I was on at the Bank. It would mean I would have to stop saving for my mortgage and seriously rethink my outgoings. But it could be done. I forced myself to focus on the bigger picture. It could mean my career wasn't over, even if I had to take a step back in pay.

The next day I met her and another director in a cafe in town. That time Steve drove me. My legs hurt from the first interview's walk and I couldn't risk limping.

I got out of the car and looked at the busy cafe. I had turned up early in hopes I would be there first. I had no idea what this woman or the guy director looked like. I walked through the doors and was hit by a wall of noise and movement. I edged over to the left-hand side by the serving area and took out my phone to try and look busy. I hoped I gave off the aura of waiting for someone, so people wouldn't approach me, except for these directors.

A woman with blonde hair approached me. 'Rosie?'

I followed behind her. She was confident and well dressed, she clearly hadn't taken a pay cut anytime recently. We sat at a table that already had someone on the end. Brilliant. An interview in a bustling cafe, next to some stranger who would hear everything.

I sat and desperately tried to block out the background noise, focusing on her movements and actions. She smiled at me and launched into introductions. She talked really enthusiastically and so fast. The other director would be turning up late was what she was explaining.

I nodded. No, Rosie, you couldn't do non-verbal shit. You had to find words.

'Okay, yeah that's fine. No problem,' I responded.

We started discussing my role at the Bank and my past before that. I tried to be as honest as possible about why I wanted to leave the bank, that the hours and pressure were a lot. I explained how I wanted to return to more accounting roots. She smiled at me and I felt a wave of safety wash over me. She seemed to understand me. Was that possible? She barely knew me.

About ten minutes into our conversation the male director showed up. He was sharply dressed but soft in his demeanour. After the woman director did the introductions, he asked a question I loved answering, 'What made you want to be an accountant?'

I smiled at him as I answered 'I fell in love with accounting when I was seventeen years old. I did an accounting module in college that I loved. Then when I got 100% in the exam, I realised it isn't very often in life that what you love and what you are good at align so clearly. I decided to pursue accounting.'

He smiled back at me. 'Good answer.'

I didn't need to fake that answer. I had given everything from that point at seventeen until the interview moment to become an accountant. As my journey has shown, a bit too much at times. But no one could ever doubt, even this sharply dressed managing director, that I loved accountancy.

The interview came to a close and I set off to head home. I put one unsteady foot in front of the other and slowly made my way home.

The next day my phone lit up with the director's name. I tried to steady my voice as I answered, 'hello?'

'Hi Rosie. I want to offer you the accounting job, at the same salary you are currently on,' she stated.

The same salary. Based on my CV she was offering lower than my current salary but based on meeting me she would match the higher amount. I was worth more on paper, I was always worth more on paper. How is it possible that after meeting me someone would see more value?

'The role will sit behind the accountants that are hands-on with clients. It will be reconciliations and work without using the phones. More of a back-office role,' she explained.

I accepted the role and agreed to send her further

admin information over so she could get the contract ready. I put the phone down and leaned back in my chair. I was a big believer in everything happening for a reason, but that was insane.

The next week I received my contract and made a meeting on Friday with my manager at the Bank. I needed to hand in my notice. It was all happening so fast. Just weeks ago I had been advised by the doctor to leave the Bank.

'Thank you for everything. For all the support the Bank has given me,' I started to say but my manager cut over me —

'You did it all yourself, Rosie,' he said, echoing Jake's words months earlier. 'You are a valued member of this team.'

'I'll come back off sick leave on Monday and work my notice. To give a full handover of my accounts,' I explained.

'You don't need to do that, you know? You have nothing to feel guilty about if you are off for your notice period,' he said.

'No, it's fine. I want to. I need to do it properly,' I answered. 'Is it okay if I see Zac before I head off today?'

'Of course. He'd love to see you,' he smiled.

Zac and I spoke regularly, and he already knew the outcome of the doctors and everything that had happened. But I hadn't told him I was interviewing for somewhere new. I walked in and saw him sat at his desk. I smiled at the sight of him. When I started at the Bank, I knew it would be me against the system. What I never expected was to find a friend along the way. To find a guy that could bring light to an often dark period of my life.

I sat in my empty seat beside him. He turned and grinned as he saw it was me.

'Alright, ditcher. Come back for some top bants, have we?' he joked.

I smiled at him. God I would miss him.

'Of course. Life isn't the same without the banter legend,' I grinned at him. 'I just handed in my notice… I'll be back on Monday to work it out.'

He didn't seem surprised. I think part of him saw it coming. He knew more than anyone the toll that the Bank had taken on me.

My notice period passed quicker than I would have liked. I walked out of the building for the last time and looked back. A part of me longed to stay at the Bank. No matter what it had put me through, what it had taken from me, it was still the job that proved I could work. I was immensely proud of everything I had achieved there.

FRANK

On Monday morning my alarm went off at 7:30 a.m., a lie in compared to the Bank. I headed out to walk to work. The walk was quiet as the town centre was pretty empty at that time, no bustling shoppers.

The office was big, but it was nothing on the Bank. My first day would be spent shadowing others and learning different roles.

I was sitting with the head of tax when she asked what it was like working for the Bank.

'Intense. Long hours and you couldn't go until your accounts were done,' I answered.

'Yeah, there's nothing like that here. Everyone goes on time,' she said.

I smiled at her. I wasn't sure if she was joking or not.

After speaking to the head of tax I was to sit with someone from sales. Salespeople weren't exactly my go to; all that confidence and arrogance wasn't something I was particularly drawn to. I reluctantly headed over to sit next to her.

I sat awkwardly between the saleswoman and the person to the desk beside her, not quite enough space for me to get out of the way of those walking by.

'The company is split into the different departments. But the sales can come in at any point and feed into the different areas,' she began. She launched into the theory behind the sales department and how it intertwined with the other departments, from the tax division to the Small to Medium Enterprise section and Limited Companies. I watched in awe as the explained the logic that underpinned her role and how she approached her sales.

Before that moment, sales was a mystery to me. People that could not only comfortably talk to others, but do it for a living, made no sense to me and quite honestly scared me. But as she looked me in the eye I realised, she didn't scare me. Someone walked behind and I instinctively pulled away, and closer to the saleswoman. Huh, guess she was safe. Not exactly what I would have predicted for my first day.

She finished up by demonstrating how she handled a sales call. I sat there in amazement at how someone could nonchalantly work their way through a call, while strategizing how to direct it. People are quick to question my academic results and how I manage to achieve them, but what she was doing was a skill I would never have and could never study. For the first time I saw her with her strengths, and me with mine. We worked for the same company and were completely different, yet we both brought value to the table. After all, a team of people with the same skill set, really wouldn't be a very successful team. Eleven world class strikers wouldn't win a world cup.

I was sitting at my desk looking through accounts and familiarising myself with the new software when 5:30 p.m. hit. As it hit everyone in the office stood up. I looked around surprised. What was happening? Impromptu dance routine?

They all started to head out of the office. I quickly closed everything off and got my stuff.

I guessed that tax woman wasn't kidding. Did I get to leave at exactly 5:30 p.m. every single day? I would get home at the same time every day. I would have a… a routine.

Over the next few days I settled into this new regimented routine of 9 a.m. start and 5:30 p.m. finish. Until Thursday morning, when I realised maybe there was no such thing as the perfect job for me.

I was sitting at my desk when the printer started going behind me. That was okay, it wouldn't last long. The machine across to my left then kicked in. Okay, that one was louder. The two combined created a roar of noise coming from behind and beside me. A few minutes later and the noise continued. I could feel it bashing at the inside of my brain. My fingers pushed against themselves as I felt myself reaching the tipping point of sensory overload. I could no longer see my screen as my eyes lost focus.

I got up and made my way to the toilets. I shut the door behind me and sat on the toilet lid. Was this working life for me? Recovering from sensory overload in bathrooms. I waited as I calmed down and felt a better sense of control. Hopefully the machines would stop if I waited it out.

I walked back into the office to its usual rumble of noise, the machines had thankfully stopped. I looked at my hands. Well, that wouldn't be great if it happened a lot.

That Friday I walked into the office and settled into my desk.

'Morning, Rosie,' said the head of tax.

I smiled. She had said morning to me every day that week. I didn't always reply. Some days I forgot to plan to reply to her, still shocked at someone saying it each day. Some days I did reply. She was easy to talk to. What kind of weird wizardry was going on with the new company? I had never felt so comfortable with a group of strangers in my life.

The next Thursday the same thing happened. The machines kicked in and I fell into sensory overload and subsequent recovery in the bathroom. I decided to do something about it. I would not fight through a workday anymore. Later that day I had a catch up with my director. I would see if I could take an early lunch when the machine was being used.

In the meeting I explained the situation honestly. Nobody ever understands sensory overload.

Everybody always thinks we are overreacting. Maybe I should bang the machine on the inside of their skull and see how they like it.

'You can do whatever works for you. Take lunch, wear headphones, whatever you need,' she answered.

Okay. Maybe I wouldn't bash the inside of her skull with the machine. She seemed to want to make it easier for me.

The next day I walked in and took my usual seat, getting into the rhythm of my new routine.

'Where has the franking machine gone?' someone in the tax team asked.

What on earth was a franking machine? Had they named a machine Frank? Bit strange.

I looked over to where the question had come from. They were stood to my left. They were stood by the horrible loud machine. Except they weren't, because the table was empty.

'It's been moved to the conference room. Not sure why,' the head of tax called back.

My mouth fell open in shock. She had moved the machine. She had moved the loud machine into a separate room, so it wouldn't push me to sensory overload each week. She wasn't a boss full of talk. She was someone who acted on her words. She had seen something causing me a problem and fixed it. I could trust her.

I sat back in my chair and looked over my PC monitors at the words written across the wall:

Exchequer Accountancy. I smiled as I took in the moment. I had made it. I was exactly where I was supposed to be.

REAR-VIEW MIRROR

Would I go back and warn myself off this path, if I could? Would I tell myself that the price would be too high, and that the accounting dream would cost too much?

No. I wouldn't.

If I hadn't taken that path, I wouldn't have found Exchequer.

If I hadn't taken that path, I wouldn't have the profound appreciation for walking that I have now.

If I hadn't taken that path, I wouldn't have met one of the best humans on the planet: Zac.

If I hadn't taken that path, I wouldn't have met Christine. She proved to me that I could fall in love. If you got confused about us throughout the story, then you understood perfectly. We never made any sense, not to others and certainly not to ourselves. We burned intensely and, most of the time, uncontrollably. Just after starting at Exchequer I found peace in accepting that we weren't very good for each other, not in the long term. I deliberately held back on detailing our friendship as it is not just my story to tell. We parted ways but I will always love her, and she will always be the girl who proved I am capable of falling in love.

I believe everything happens for a reason. Those things needed to happen for me to end up where I am today.

I write this having worked at the accounting firm, Exchequer, for over a year.

I made some poor choices along the way, there is no denying that. But hasn't everyone? I was naive and focused so much on my career that it nearly cost me my health.

I spent many years being a square peg and trying to bash myself into a round hole, no matter what it cost me. No matter what parts of myself I would have to lose- to fit in. I now realise I never needed to change myself from being a square peg, I needed to find a home that would let me fit in, exactly as I was.

When I walked away from the Bank, I thought I was walking away from my dream. I had no idea that it was putting me on a new path, to a different dream.

Writing.

Since starting at Exchequer, I have pursued my love of writing. I have written for the National Autistic Society as well as various magazines and organisations. I run a blog on which I share my life experiences as an autistic adult and someone who has faced mental health problems.

Ironically, finding Exchequer- allowed me to find

who I was, away from accountancy. Without my accounting career dominating my life I have had the freedom to be who I was always meant to be.

Rosie Weldon.
Accountant, and writer.

THANKYOU

I wouldn't be where I am today without being lucky enough to have stumbled across some fantastic people.

A few thank yous (by no means an exhaustive list):

To Mum — For fighting my corner when I didn't have the strength to.

To Charlie — For always saying the right thing at the right time. For being my big brother.

To Steve — For being the best taxi driver around. Kidding. You came into my life to protect and care for Mum and Jenson. Somewhere along the road you became one of my biggest protectors.

To Jess and Jamie — For doing all the little things that didn't make the book. Ordering my drinks before I have to ask. Going with me to appointments. None of it goes unnoticed.

To Craig — For understanding what no one else in my life could.

To Harry James Potter — For always being there.

To Siana — For being the most understanding best friend.

To 'Christine' — For proving the impossible was possible, that I could fall in love. For putting up with me while life kept knocking me down.

To 'Jake' — For believing in me when I didn't. My whole career is because of you. No, don't say it's not. Your belief in me burns within me to this day.

To 'Ashley' — For never asking me to change.

To 'Lena' — For being on my side when no one else at university was. For standing up for me. For changing the course of my life.

To 'Zac' — For being my rock. For being my biggest supporter.

To 'Lucy' — For telling me to go back.

To Exchequer — For being my safe place. For proving I can belong somewhere.

To Jenson — For being my reason.

To you — For picking this book up and coming along for the journey. The support my writing has received is incredible. If you wish to know what happened after this book ends, come find me:

Website: www.rosieweldon.com
Twitter: www.twitter.com/rosieweldon18
Facebook: www.facebook.com/rosieweldon118
Instagram: www.instagram.com/rosie__weldon

Printed in Great Britain
by Amazon